Tiger Cub

A 74 Squadron Fighter Pilot in World War II

To the Tigers who were lost
but not forgotten

Tiger Cub

A 74 Squadron Fighter Pilot in World War II

The Story of John Connell Freeborn DFC*

by

Christopher Yeoman

Pen & Sword
AVIATION

First Published in Great Britain in 2009 by
Pen & Sword Aviation
an imprint of
Pen & Sword Books Ltd
47 Church Street, Barnsley, South Yorkshire S70 2AS

ISBN 978-1-84884-023-2

A CIP catalogue record for this book is
available from the British Library.

Typeset in 11/13pt Palatino by
Concept, Huddersfield

Printed and bound in England by
CPI UK

Pen & Sword Books Ltd incorporates the Imprints of Pen & Sword Aviation,
Pen & Sword Maritime, Pen & Sword Military, Wharncliffe Local History,
Pen & Sword Select, Pen & Sword Military Classics, Leo Cooper,
Remember When, Seaforth Publishing and Frontline Publishing.

For a complete list of Pen & Sword titles please contact
PEN & SWORD BOOKS LIMITED
47 Church Street, Barnsley, South Yorkshire, S70 2AS, England
E-mail: enquiries@pen-and-sword.co.uk
Website: www.pen-and-sword.co.uk

Contents

Foreword

I have had the privilege of knowing Wing Commander John Freeborn for at least fifteen years. Our initial meeting came about through the 74 (F) Tiger Squadron Association when he first became a member together with Peta, his much missed wife. I had previously been trying to contact John during the course of my researches for *Tigers*, my history of the Squadron, published to celebrate its 75th Anniversary, but he had been living in Spain and my enquiries led to dead ends. Thus I wasn't able to include any of his recollections in that particular book. I was consequently delighted when he returned to the UK and we decided to tell his story in a new book. This led to *A Tiger's Tale* which covered John's complete RAF career.

Now Chris Yeoman has written *Tiger Cub*, concentrating solely on John's time as a Tiger. Despite his connections with other squadrons (including command of 118) during the wartime years, 74 – the legendary Tigers – is the Squadron to which John always feels he owes the greatest allegiance. He is extremely proud to have flown and fought with it when he did. Today all members of the very active Squadron Association recognise that in John they have in their midst one of the great names of the Battle of Britain. Each year at the Squadron Reunion (which John always attends) they demonstrate that by their absolute pleasure at his being there. They are inestimably proud of him and as proud of the fact that he is proud of the Squadron! When a few years ago he was asked to speak after the dinner, he was given a standing ovation. That is a measure of the respect in which he is held.

John now refers to himself with a twinkle in his eye as being amongst the 'Last of the Few'. We can never repay the debt we owe to him and his colleagues except by ensuring their stories are told and thus are never forgotten, especially as the number of Battle of Britain pilots diminishes as the passing of time takes its toll. John is regularly in demand to attend promotional events across the country – usually for book and print signings – and he travels considerable distances to support those of them he can. His age seems to be no barrier to his commitment to doing so and he passionately believes that it is important that while he is able to he must continue to tell his story and thereby the story of the RAF during those critical times. It is therefore so very appropriate that Chris has decided to write this book which has the same objective.

Tiger Cub is written in an accessible novel-like style that serves to make John's story all the more immediate. It is not always a heroic story recounting tales of derring-do, for life on 74 wasn't always harmonious and personality clashes were commonplace, as were problems caused by the perceived gulf between commissioned and non-commissioned officers. John was one amongst several who was never able to suffer fools gladly: and he was always one to speak his mind, then and now. But he was always the consummate professional who put differences aside because the Squadron as a whole was more important than the individuals within it.

Read this book and appreciate once again what we owe to all those who fought in the Battle of Britain and beyond. They were young men who sacrificed their youth – and very often their lives – in defence of their country. Furthermore the telling of John's story is also the story of a great Squadron during one of its finest periods. Chris has done a fine job in recreating for us how it was to have been a Tiger from 1938–1941. Enjoy.

Bob Cossey
Norwich

Acknowledgements

I would like to express my gratitude to John Freeborn for the encouragement and enthusiasm he has offered during the writing of this book and for the countless hours he has spent retelling his wonderful stories and experiences to me in his home and on the telephone. I really appreciate his brilliant sense of humour and for his unwavering boldness and conviction. I would like to thank Derek Morris, Tony Pickering and Ron Duckenfield for contributing to this story and Michael Robinson for his assistance regarding research, photographs and squadron information. I also want to thank 74 (F) Tiger Squadron Association, Bob Cossey and E M Aitken for contributing their photographs to this book. I would like to offer my thanks to David Pritchard for his outstanding artwork and Wilf Crutchley and Alan Johnson for their assistance throughout this project. I would also like to offer my deep appreciation to my father, Bob Yeoman, firstly for introducing me to John and secondly, for turning my eyes away from Tornados and Typhoons and towards Spitfires and Hurricanes. I am ever grateful for his support and belief in this work. Last but not least, I would like to thank my wife, Kym, for being patient with the dozens of cassette tapes, letters, books, combat reports and pictures scattered around our home and for always encouraging me to follow my dreams.

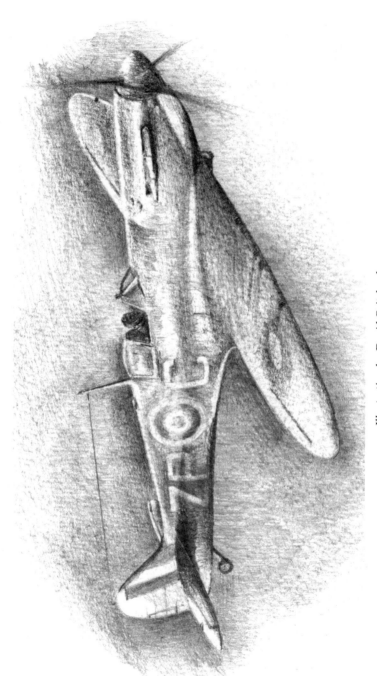

Illustration by David Pritchard

Prologue

The dark green Junkers Ju 87G-2 'Stuka' stood motionless in the dimly lit hanger. The static, black propeller blades sported fingerprints, breaking up the thin layer of dust that had settled. The open polished cockpits were empty, the exhausts clean and the 7.92mm machine guns rendered useless. After being captured by British troops in Germany 1945, this vulture-like war bird now rested from its labours, never to wail the *Jericho-Trompete* again. 'That was the easiest one to knock down' John said sitting in a wheelchair whilst looking over the Stuka's white undercarriage and yellow-tipped wings with thick black crosses painted onto them. I crouched down beside him and he nodded towards the dive bomber, telling me they were easy pickings during the summer of 1940 due to their low speed and lack of armour.

It was a beautiful sunny afternoon as I pushed John in a wheelchair we had borrowed from the RAF Hendon museum across the road towards the Battle of Britain hall. The museum was fairly quiet by now. On our way to the aircraft exhibits we passed Ken Wilkinson of 616 Squadron and Tony Pickering of 501 Squadron. They were standing in front of a Hurricane wreck and were quietly talking amongst themselves. John looked at the wreckage for a moment and asked me what it was. 'That's what's left of a Hurricane' I said. 'Poor Bugger' John replied and we entered the Battle of Britain hall, stopping at the Ju 87 'Stuka'. While I was crouched down beside John, listening to him talk about the Stuka, I looked down at his black jumper and smiled at the 74 'Tiger' Squadron insignia proudly worn on his chest. Here I was, in the Battle of Britain hall at Hendon with Wing Commander John Connell Freeborn in June 2007.

John was at Hendon for the weekend as a special guest for the 'Legends Aviation Gallery'. He had spent the weekend talking with enthusiasts and non enthusiasts alike; signing their books, prints and anything else they wanted his florid signature on. This marked the third event I had spent with John and by far the most memorable.

As we neared the large Junkers Ju 88R-1 John looked up at me with a slight grin, pointed at the beast and said in his gruff voice 'That was a bloody bastard to get down.' I smiled and inquired further. 'Oh yes' he said 'No matter how many bursts you put in, it didn't seem to make a bloody scratch.' I looked over at the Bf 109E-3 and thought to myself what a terrible opponent that must have been. I gazed at its bright yellow nose and slick airframe with interest and respect. I turned to John who seemed unaware of its presence and directed his attention to the exceptional aeroplane. I wondered what was running through his mind. Was it strange to see all these years later? Did it stir up any feelings long forgotten? Surely it must be slightly un-nerving because the Messerschmitt Bf 109 was a formidable fighter? Continuing to look at the 109, I asked 'How about that John?' John looked at the fighter as if it was barely even there, his face expression calm and unmoved. Then suddenly he looked at me and retorted 'That was a crap aeroplane.' He paused for a moment to gauge my reaction. We looked at each other, laughed and then turned around to face the Hurricane and Spitfire.

Whenever I see these magnificent historical aircraft they never fail to catch my imagination, filling me with wonder and not to mention a great deal of pleasure, but for John Freeborn these feelings are absent and why shouldn't they be? After all, John flew in and amongst these spectacular war machines in the greatest and deadliest air battles ever fought.

CHAPTER ONE

Early Life

It was 10 o'clock on a Sunday evening when the young man arrived at Hornchurch. Standing 5ft 6 inches tall, with neat, short dark brown hair and bright blue eyes, Acting Pilot Officer John Freeborn reported to Hornchurch on the 29 October, 1938. As an A Class Reservist, John was posted from Flying Training School (FTS) to join the already acclaimed 74 'Tiger' Squadron at eighteen years of age. Located in east London, Hornchurch was then commanded by Group Captain Walkington. One of the very first people John met when he arrived at the station was none other than Bob Stanford Tuck of 65 Squadron. After a few welcoming beers, Tuck gave the new recruit a tour of the aerodrome's buildings, facilities and finally the airfield. As they strolled into the night, John looked out across the aerodrome and quietly wondered what the coming months held in store for him. There was an unsettling undercurrent of war in the air and in John's mind it wasn't a matter of 'if' but 'when?' Nevertheless, for now here he was, serving in one of the greatest squadrons the Royal Air Force had to offer and what an incredible addition he would eventually become. The new tiger cub of 74 would soon grow into one of the most dynamic, courageous and fiercest fighters the squadron, in fact the RAF, would ever have.

As in many successful units throughout the military, the men who served in the infamous 74 'Tiger' Squadron during the Second World War came from different backgrounds, different parts of the country and even different parts of the world.

John Connell Freeborn was born on 1 December 1919 in Middleton, North Yorkshire. John's mother, Jean, was a stern Scottish woman, a straight talker with a firm countenance. 'I never saw her smile' John said when speaking of his mother. The photograph taken of Jean and her smartly dressed son after he received the Distinguished Flying Cross (DFC) will testify of that too! She was a hard woman that rarely showed any emotions and even though at times she found it difficult to tolerate John's two sisters she was very supportive and protective of her children. John's father, Harold Freeborn was a hard working bank manager with the Yorkshire Penny Bank. He was a strict disciplinarian who possessed a big stick. John and his three brothers were often acquainted with it when they stepped over the mark. The Freeborn's regularly attended their local Church of England parish church each Sunday. Jean and Harold would sit on the end of the pew with their children next to them, running down in age order, all dressed in their Sunday best. On one such occasion John leant over to his younger brother, their eyes following the collection plate. 'When it comes over Brian, grab a handful' John said in a whisper with a slight grin. As the tray neared, Brian took a fistful of money and in a matter of mere seconds Harold's big stick was raised. He thundered it down onto Brian's hand causing him to wince. As he did, the tray fell and crashed down onto the floor with an almighty sound, spilling money everywhere. 'Right then' John thought, leaping down and helping himself to the scattered coins on the ground whilst Brian got sharp looks and a firm talking to. John sat back down feeling pleased with the generous donations he had acquired from the good saints and pretended to enjoy the rest of the service. However, to John's disappointment he was vigorously searched at the end of church and had to return his precious findings. John chuckled to himself as he remembered that old stick his Father used to wield. 'He whacked me with it several times' John recalls, 'but I was ever grateful for the discipline he instilled in me ... discipline that I would need all those years later.'

Despite the tough regulation in the Freeborn household and the unwavering order in the siblings rearing, they led a comfortable life. Together they would enjoy summer holidays spent in Bridlington. John's favoured and now treasured moments as a youngster was when his father would take him to the Railways. Together they would watch the magnificent steam trains chug along the tracks and ever since then John has been extremely fond of them.

In due course the Freeborns left the lovely open farming area of Middleton and moved to Headingley. It was here that John attended the Leeds Grammar School and to his great annoyance it was an unpleasant time. John quickly began to loath the authoritarian nature of certain figures at the School, especially when their severe actions were unmerited. To this day, John is a man that does not suffer fools gladly. He is confident in what is right and never flinches to speak his mind honestly, bluntly and without hesitation. Even at 87 years of age, John is sharp as a button and strong in his convictions. With this in mind it comes as no surprise to learn that John slugged his teacher after being repeatedly hit over the head with the edge of a ruler. Teacher and student ended up on the floor with fists flying and teeth gnashing. Naturally, Harold was informed of his boy's exploits but the steadfastness of his father was something John could always rely upon. When Harold learnt of the situation he stood in his son's corner with full support, relieving him of any further consequences. It was examples like this which caused John to have great respect and adoration towards his father.

There was no love lost when the blue-eyed boy left School at age sixteen. He found the system difficult to adjust to, always feeling like they were two opposing forces. By now he was well accustomed to the use of rules and discipline, having seen both its constructive and unnecessary effects in his early years. John believes that these diverse experiences, especially his upbringing, all aided in arming him for his future responsibilities in the RAF. John speaks fondly of his parents when reflecting upon his youth, feeling appreciative of their tough nurture. Whether he felt that way as a young lad remains to be uncovered.

Like most young men, John now wrestled with the universal question of 'What on earth am I going to do now?' His father hoped that John would follow in his footsteps and join him at the bank, but John decided it just wasn't an option for him. With little or no desire to continue his studies he was faced with a choice between working in the coal mines and joining the armed services. John elected for the latter. Initially he had wanted to join the Royal Navy so he applied to be an Artificer's Apprentice but failed the exam. Then not long after John saw an RAF Reserve of Air Force Officers advert in the newspaper and thought he'd try his luck. At the age of seventeen he was accepted. John began by performing the duties of drummer and bugle boy in the Officer Training Corps (OTC) but soon decided that for the first time in his life he wanted to fly. John kept noticing recruiting adverts appearing in the Yorkshire Post which soon began to stir him with interest. At this time John had never really given flying much thought, in fact he had never even been close to an aeroplane before, but having looked into it he decided to apply anyway. 'I thought – I'll try and learn to fly, get paid for it and if I don't like it I'll bugger off.' Like any caring mother, Jean wasn't thrilled with the idea of her son taking to the skies. When she caught John reading through the application forms one day she inquired. 'What are those you've got?' 'They're forms for joining the air force' John replied. 'You're not joining any air force! I didn't bring you up for that; you'll get a proper job.' As John continued to read through the forms he decided not to take any notice of what his mother had to say. 'I found it most interesting.'

After filling out the forms, John excitedly sent them off with a hopeful heart. He wondered how long he would have to wait, but mercifully the wait was short lived and John was soon instructed to go to London, where he would stand before a commissioning board. 'Off to London I went accompanied by my father, who made it a lot better for me. I was only seventeen and so I couldn't go alone. I went to a commissioning board made up of people from all walks of life, not air force at all. They fired questions at me at a terrific rate, questions ranging from maths to locomotive engines. Eventually the questions came at me so fast that I began to lose track of what I was saying.' After doing his very best to respond to the firing squad John was sent out of the room where he sat nervously waiting for the outcome. Soon enough the youngster was brought back before the board and told he was to have a medical. 'But I've got my father waiting outside,' John said considerately. 'Well let him wait. You shouldn't be concerned about him.' So off John went to have a medical. It was intense and it seemed to last for hours, until finally they said he could leave. Feeling relieved, John made his way towards the exit where he was greeted by his father. 'What happened, are you in?' Harold asked his son with eagerness. 'No, they're going to let me know,' John said glumly. 'But I don't think I've passed the medical.' John had a terrible cold that day which prevented him from holding his breath for the full minute that was required. John remembers, 'You couldn't cheat it because they put a clip on your nose and you couldn't breathe through your mouth because they'd see. Anyway, I couldn't do it and so they told me to come back in a week's time. I practiced holding my breath until I was blue in the face.' A week later, much to his mother's displeasure, John passed the medical. She said, 'If you want to be a bloody fool and go and kill yourself, you better go and learn to fly.' So off John went.

On 17 January 1938, John made his way to the Elementary Flying Training School (EFTS) at Sywell. 'My father and brother took me to the station. My brother was a strong lad being a farmer so he carried my suitcase that my mother had carefully packed for me. When we got there I told them that I'd be fine from here and that they could go, so they did. While I was alone three blokes came along and started picking on me. They started saying things like 'Oh daddy's boy! Did daddy have to come and see you off at the station?' so I thought 'you shouldn't be saying these things' and I got stuck in and bloody belted them. Eventually I arrived at Sywell and much to my surprise I saw one of them there, looking just as surprised to see me. He said to his mate 'Watch him, he'll knock your bloody teeth out if you look at him.'

As it happened John never had any more trouble from the likes of Mickey-takers at Sywell and in any case, 'That useless bugger got thrown off the course because he couldn't fly.' The EFTS was equipped with the reliable and favoured biplane, the Tiger Moth. Designed by de Havilland, the Tiger Moth biplane was introduced in the early 1930s and remained in service with the RAF until 1952. With a range of 300 miles, a service ceiling of 13,600 feet and a maximum speed of 109mph, the Tiger Moth was used by the RAF as a primary two-seater trainer. It was here at Sywell that John first saw the aircraft up close. Standing 8 feet and 9 inches tall off the ground with a length of 23 feet and 11 inches, John studied the flimsy looking structure and began to feel less enthusiastic about his chosen career path. 'I thought this is a joke isn't it? That doesn't fly, the bloody clapped out old thing.' But John was shaken from his thoughts as he heard the instructor shouting at him from behind. 'GET IN!' John climbed into the front seat of the Tiger Moth and began to settle himself down. Again, the instructor's voice bellowed towards him. 'You don't sit in the front! I sit there!' John thought, 'Oh dear, oh dear, what a nasty gentlemen. I'm not going to like this.'

After a baffling introduction to the Tiger Moth's cockpit and instruments, John climbed into the backseat like a bag of nerves. The noisy engine suddenly awoke from its slumber. John made sure he was securely strapped in and as the 'marvellous little aeroplane' trotted off down the runway, the butterflies in John's stomach began to flutter. The instructor taxied across the grass and then he turned the Tiger Moth into wind. 'How do I know I've turned into wind?' the instructor asked his pupil. 'I don't know,' John replied. 'Well look at the bloody windsock then!' 'Oh yes,' John said, 'but I didn't even know what the blasted thing was'.

Then, in no time at all they were up, they were flying! The instructor began to climb and John began to feel more at ease and thought, 'If it stays like this I'll be alright', but of course it didn't.

At 7,000ft the instructor broke the silence. 'Now, I'm going to show you things.' He said gleefully. John knew what was coming so he quickly began to search around the cockpit for something to grab a hold of. 'There's nothing to hold ...' the instructor said looking in the mirror. '... just sit still and enjoy it because you're going to have to do it for me shortly. The first thing we do is stall the aircraft', the instructor said pulling the nose of the Tiger Moth up until it wouldn't go any further. Then suddenly the nose dropped and down they went like a heavy stone towards the earth. John's stomach didn't agree with the manoeuvre but he managed to hold himself together. Then finally, the instructor levelled the Tiger Moth out and John thought the worst was now behind him.

'The next thing we're going to do is a spin.' The instructor announced. John thought, 'No, we're not going to do a spin. He's kidding me, this will all come later.' But it didn't, it came immediately! The instructor pulled the nose up again, pulled hard on the stick, kicked in left rudder and off they went into a spin. 'It's really easy to get out of a spin'. The instructor shouted, '... you straighten your rudder and the nose stops turning and then you ease back on the stick to level out.' And sure enough, that's exactly what he did.

During John's initiation flight the instructor professionally did all the Tiger Moth was capable of to show the young student what he was in for. The biplane was put through the motions. They spun, looped, stalled and recovered, making it a terrifying experience for the unfamiliar passenger. Reflecting upon this experience John refers to it as 'terrible' but agrees that the instructor had to welcome newcomers to the world of aviation in this manner to prepare them for every possible sensation an aircraft would give them.

After an hour of flying the Tiger Moth finally touched down on the grass aerodrome and John was relieved. However, not long after his first adventure in the sky, John quickly became accustomed to the sensations of flying and began to thoroughly enjoy it.

The training course was carried out by Brooklands Aviation, a civilian company that was contracted by the RAF. The course lasted for three months, enabling the students to gain 50 hours worth of flying time. One week they would fly in the mornings and then spend the afternoons in classroom instruction and then the next week the schedule would be reversed. On average, after 7 to 8 hours of flying with an instructor students would be permitted to fly solo depending on their progression. After only 4 hours and 20 minutes, John Freeborn went solo. He was rated as an 'above average' pilot but later began to struggle in the classroom. After being informed that he wasn't doing very well, three of his friends took action. Jack Caslaw, 'Butch' Surtess and Ron Courtenay made it a personal mission to ensure that John would work extra hard on his studies. As John dedicated himself to the task at hand, his chums convinced the instructors that he should take the exam early. The instructors agreed to the request and John successfully passed the exam. The very fact that the instructors allowed this to happen just goes to show the faith they must have had in John's abilities as a pilot. Other than John's fellow accomplices, this special exception didn't sit well with the other students, as John could now sit back and relax in the sure knowledge he had made it, while the rest of the students worried their way through their own exams. John remembers, 'I had a lot of fun because while the others were doing their school work, I was flying, but I dare not say anything to them, because in the emergency water tank I'd go. I think I spent more time in that water tank than I did in the air.'

Flying was not the only thing John and his peers learned at the training school. 'We learnt how to chase the girls ... and I did remarkably well when I was at Sywell.' John remembers spending a lot of time with a 'pleasant young girl' often swimming in the evenings or spending time at the railway tracks together. John soon warmed up to his new lady friend, Margaret, but found she was good at playing 'hard to get'. One night at the railway tracks John brought a firework along with him. John thought, 'When the express comes past, she won't hear me flick my lighter and so I'll light the firework and set it off'. The firework gave an almighty bang and she literally jumped into John's arms. John remembers that, 'Margaret was a very nice girl that enjoyed my company and I enjoyed hers, but things never happen the way you would like them to do.'

John's romance with Margaret rapidly elevated to a level which he was uncomfortable with. She began asking him if they were going to get married and at that time John couldn't have thought of anything worse. 'For a start my mother would have bloody killed me if she knew what was going on'. Fortunately for John his three months at Sywell came to an end and he escaped to Montrose.

John picks up the story:

> *She wrote to me at Montrose but I threw the letter away because I had no interest in marriage. Jack Caslaw was engaged at the time so he'd go back to Northampton at the weekends and he'd run into Margaret. One day he said to me, 'I keep seeing this girl you know and she keeps asking about you'. 'Well, tell her I crashed into the north sea', I said. 'Right I'll tell her', Jack said and when he next saw her in Northampton she asked 'Did you give John my message? Did you tell him to write to me?' Jack said, 'Oh it's a shame about John. He'd write to you but he can't, he's dead, went into the North Sea'. Sadly, poor Margaret broke down and I thought what a rotten bugger I was to do a thing like that.*

The keen young pupil was now stationed at No. 8 Flying Training School (FTS) at Montrose. The FTS were using the 'lovely Hawker Hart' as a two-seater trainer. The Hawker Hart had a lot more advantages over the Tiger Moth. First of all it was somewhat larger, achieving a range of 430 miles, a speed of 168 mph and a climbing height of 22,800 feet. The Hawker Hart was an impressive biplane. 'Its fuselage looked very similar to its successor, the Hawker Hurricane'.

At Montrose a new and frightening aspect of training was required: blind flying. A hood was used to block out the pilot's vision, therefore the pilot would have to rely fully upon the aircrafts instruments. Blind flying was an unsettling experience but extremely necessary in preparing the pilot for night flying. During John's stay at FTS he was rigorously trained in reconnaissance work, cross-country navigation flying and air-gunnery training which took place at the Air Firing School (AFS) at Catfoss. The AFS's programme included dive-bombing training and air firing which was aimed at drogues towed by Fairy Swordfish. The pupils' bullets were dipped in paint to mark their hits.

John achieved 15% accuracy, the average was 7%. Another less interesting but essential part of training was learning the proper self conduct and protocol used in the RAF. John thoroughly enjoyed his time at Montrose, eventually gaining his wings as an 'above average' pilot.

During this period of training, German *Luftwaffe* pilots like Galland, Schellmann and Mölders were already chalking up victories in the Condor Legion and gaining valuable combat experience in the Spanish Civil War. Germany was rapidly acquiring beneficial knowledge on air warfare tactics in addition to testing and improving the performance of their aircraft. It had only been a few years previously that Hitler had unveiled the strength of the new *Luftwaffe*, spurring the RAF to organise themselves in a panicked hurry. The RAF wisely divided itself into sections of Fighter, Bomber, Coastal and Training commands. Squadrons and Training Schools were largely increased and opportunities for short-service commissions were widely available.

In July 1936, Sir Hugh Dowding became commander-in-chief of Fighter Command and swiftly began to work on Britain's defences, expertly incorporating the early-warning radar system as well as integrating the Observer Corps. Meanwhile across the channel, Germany continued to rearm and Britain desperately struggled to fortify herself.

As the faint, distant echoes of the war drums sounded, John hoped with all his might that he would be posted to a Fighter Squadron. Only the fastest and most modern aircraft the RAF had to offer could satisfy such a young pilot's desires. Fortunately for John and for Fighter Command his silent pleas were heard. After his training at Montrose concluded, John Freeborn was posted to 74 Squadron based at Hornchurch.

There was a slight chill in the October air. The handsome, fresh-faced John Freeborn was on the brink of war and he knew it. Standing next to the lean figure of Bob Tuck he felt incredibly young to be there ... and he was.

CHAPTER TWO

Hornchurch

The aerodrome at Hornchurch was a splendid station with grass runways and brick buildings. It was established in 1915 for the purpose of preventing German air raids over Britain. Originally a site on Sutton's farm, the Air Ministry purchased the area as well as some adjacent land due to its ideal location, allowing adequate defence of the Eastern approach to London. In due time the site was expanded and on 1 April 1928, it was opened as an RAF aerodrome. Eight years later Hornchurch became part of No. 11 Group in Fighter Command. It seemed a long way from John's home in Headingly.

On his first night at the station John recalls.

I was soon told what I would do and what would happen ... and it happened alright, I met Bob Tuck. 'I'll fix you up with a room ...' Tuck said, '... and then we'll have a couple of beers. Have you had a drink today?' 'No ...' I said '... just a dandelion and burdock'. Tuck smiled 'Well, we'll soon put that right'. After a pleasant evening with Bob Tuck, listening to what happens and how the air force runs etc, I learnt that he was a pilot in 65 Squadron. I didn't realise we had three fighter squadrons at Hornchurch, I thought it was one fighter squadron at one aerodrome.

Squadrons, 54, 65 and 74 were stationed at Hornchurch at the time of John's posting. He was particularly pleased to be sent to 74 as it already had an outstanding reputation due to its successes in the First World War. Originally formed at Northolt on 1 July 1917, pilots such as Keith Caldwell, Mick Mannock and Ira Jones all contributed to the Squadron's achievements with their vigorous service and fighting spirit during WWI. No. 74 became known as the 'Tiger' Squadron because of their aggressiveness in the air. During the Squadron's seven month period on the front line, No. 74 had achieved 224 victories, 140 of which were confirmed, 68 probables and 15 balloons. It was later in 1936 when 74 Squadron arrived at Hornchurch that their Tiger-head badge and their 'I Fear No Man' motto was endorsed.

No. 74 Squadron was equipped with the Gloster Gauntlet when John set foot in Hornchurch. The Gauntlet was a single-seater biplane that could reach 230mph. It was faster and had a wider range than the aircraft John had previously flown which caused a great deal of excitement for the new pilot. Experience soon taught him that the Gauntlet was 'a lovely aeroplane' but certainly not the ones they had at Hornchurch! 'They were worn out ... and when I say worn out, I mean bloody worn out! The camouflaged Gauntlet's were in constant need of work and rarely serviceable'. It was frustrating for the pilots and a pain-staking task for the ground crew.

As John wandered around Hornchurch he wondered what the other Squadron members would be like. 'They were elderly pilots compared to me and when I arrived they patted me on the head and asked, "What are you doing here?" I replied "I've joined the Squadron sir!" I remember calling them all "sir" because at least I was half way there and it stopped me getting a kicking'.

The day after John's arrival he was introduced to the Squadron Adjutant, Sammy Hoare, and the senior officers. The Tigers' Commanding Officer (CO) was an Australian by the name of George 'Sammy' Sampson. He was a well regarded Squadron Leader who possessed quality leadership skills. Sampson maintained the respect of the pilots with his strict methods and 'no nonsense' attitude. John quickly took to 'Sammy' Sampson and learnt a lot from his example. 'He was like a father to me'. John remembers. 'He was a wonderful man. A fantastic controller and a good flyer too'.

A Squadron was divided into two sections: 'A' Flight and 'B' Flight. After he met the CO, John was taken over to B Flight where he would be serving. He was introduced to Flight Commander Paddy Treacy. Treacy was a tall, slender Irishman that didn't impress John in the same way his CO did. 'Treacy was a nice man when you got to know him', but at the time John thought he could be impatient, unkind and spent little time helping or warming up to the new recruits. Regardless of his shortcomings, John believes Treacy was a decent leader and a brave man. There was another Irishman in B Flight by the name of Vincent 'Paddy' Byrne who unlike Treacy was short and stocky. The two Irishman were in constant contention with each other, a contention that apparently followed them from their school in Dublin. With one being from the North of Ireland and the other the South, they just didn't get along and it often caused an uncomfortable feeling in the Flight. John liked Paddy Byrne even less than Treacy because he disliked the way he would deliberately try and wind-up Treacy.

Of course, as in all walks of life, personalities were bound to conflict, disagreements sure to occur and ill feelings expected to surface, especially when you consider the intense strains young pilots like these were under during WWII and unfortunately, due to unforeseen events Paddy Byrne was not the only Tiger John would clash with.

'A' Flight's Commander was a well built, handsome South African man called Adolph 'Sailor' Malan. By then he was in his late twenties, which was a lot older than the majority of pilots at that time and married to Lynda. In his youth Malan joined the South African Training Ship *General Botha* as a cadet and then the Union-Castle steamship line in 1927, which earned him the nickname of 'Sailor' among his fellow pilot colleagues.

On first meeting Malan, John thought he seemed nice enough and soon learnt that he was a determined leader, a fine flyer and an aggressive fighter pilot. To start with John felt the South African was a bit like Treacy in relation to the new boys but

eventually they became friends. The intelligent 'Sailor' Malan
would soon become an outstanding fighter pilot, combat tactician
and revered for his gunnery abilities. 'He was definitely the best
shot there was', John recalls, 'Without question Malan was a
brilliant marksman, but I could out fly him and I bloody told him
so too'.

To announce his arrival, John left a calling card in the Officers'
Mess and spent the next few weeks getting acquainted with the
different members of 74 Squadron. Sergeant Pilots Tony Mould,
Peter Chesters and No. 74's Training and Safety Officer Ernie
Mayne were particularly welcoming and friendly to the young
Freeborn. Gordon Heywood was another good man who treated
the new recruits very well indeed. He always made sure they
were looked after, helping them get to grips with things like
protocol and Mess conduct.

A new pilot was expected to present himself to all the married
officers within six weeks of arrival. It was the 'done thing' and 'if
the pilot failed to do it, he would be considered an unscrupulous
character!' Dressed in his best suit and maroon Tiger Squadron
tie, the anxious Pilot Officer knocked on the Station Commander's
door. Group Captain Walkington and his wife were delightful
people and kindly welcomed John to the station. After some
sherrys and light conversation, John felt a lot more at ease. It was
clearly apparent that the Tigers had a great sense of pride in their
Squadron and John felt thrilled to be a part of it.

Within the first couple of months at Hornchurch John was
sent for to see the Squadron's Adjutant. 'Have I done anything
wrong?' John asked the man sent to collect him, feeling slightly
apprehensive as they walked together. 'Don't worry boy, stand
your ground', came the reply. Not convinced, John nervously
made his way to see No. 74's Adjutant, where he was greeted by
a grinning Sammy Hoare. 'Hello Freeborn, pleased to see you.
Are you settling down well?' 'Yes sir, I'm settling down very
well thank you', John replied full of suspicion. 'Don't call me sir;
I'm only the Adjutant, same rank as you'. 'But ...' John recalls
'... He was a Pilot Officer and I was an *Acting* Pilot Officer. You
couldn't get any lower than me. Anyway, he soon put me on the
right track. Sammy Hoare was just waiting for some mug to

arrive so he could dump the job onto him and of course I hadn't been there long so that poor mug was me'. 'You're going to be the Squadron Adjutant', Hoare announced while John fought desperately hard not to look disappointed by the revelation. John was not pleased with his new position, he felt that he could barely spell let alone serve in an administrative role. Nevertheless, there was little he could do.

'Are you going to be my Adjutant Freeborn?' George Sampson asked John shortly after his visit with Sammy Hoare. 'Yes sir, I am', John replied. 'Well you don't have much say in the matter, I do all the saying around here!' So that was that! John was now 74 Squadron's Adjutant and he felt glum to say the least. However, in his new position, John would now serve alongside Squadron Leader Cooke of 65 Squadron, a man he grew very fond of. Sampson informed John that he would now be serving with Cooke on Courts of Enquiry, which generally consisted of people being brought forth for various charges and offences such as breaking out of camp and returning later than their passes permitted them to. 'You've got to try them', Sampson said to me and I thought, 'How the hell can I do that!?'

John well remembers his first incident sitting on a Court of Enquiry for a few pilots that had overstayed their passes. The Squadron Disciplinary Sergeant marched the culprits in one by one. 'Little did I know that the Squadron Disciplinary Sergeant for the airmen was a load of rubbish. No trade, no background, he was just a bully! There was nothing good about him. Now as the years go by I think how pathetic he was, how cruel, he was not what was needed to make a good fighting force. Anyway, he marched them in with caps off. ''Left, right, left, right, left, right'', and they were stood before me to account for their offences. They had only overstayed their weekend passes, really of no consequence but it gave the Disciplinary Sergeant a lot of pleasure to have these blokes got at. I listened to each story about how they missed their bus, missed their train and every other excuse and I thought, ''Now that's a shame but they're back now so Case dismissed, Case dismissed, Case dismissed.'' When it was all over Sampson approached me and he said: ''You've just let them all off!'' ''Yes sir, I didn't see any reason as to why I should say anything different. I felt sorry for them sir," John said in reply. Sampson frowned at Freeborn and said in a reprimanding tone of voice, 'We're not here to be sorry Freeborn. Don't let it happen again!'

So the following Monday comes by and again the Squadron Disciplinary Sergeant brings them into the Squadron Orderly Room and John remembers, 'It was the same old story, "I would have been back sir but this happened, or that happened", and I said, "but it happened the week before and the week before that. Twenty-eight days!" Everyone that went in after that, right or wrong, I'd say "Twenty-eight days", which meant they were confined to the camp to work in the cookhouse peeling potatoes and given all the nasty little jobs that no one wants to do, but they liked to eat so it had to be done. Again, Sampson was standing behind me and I could hear him tutting and sighing. When the court closed down and everyone had left, Sampson looked at me and said: "Freeborn, you don't know the difference between crapping and rubbing your arsehole". He just as soon threw the book at me'.

While working in this role with Squadron Leader Cooke, John came across two cases which were of a more serious nature. On one occasion they looked into a case where a Gauntlet pilot had crashed into a tree. It unfolded that he had beaten up his girlfriend's house, flew far too low and collided with a tree. The pilot broke both his legs in the accident. Another most notable case was an incident concerning that of Pilot Officer Norman Pooler. He was a friendly, good looking chap who turned up at a party one night thoroughly depressed and was seen carrying a revolver around with him. The following day he was found dead in the Mess garden. Sadly, he had shot himself in the head with a Colt 45 pistol. Squadron Leader Cooke later discovered that the Pilot Officer had contracted syphilis and was unable to cope with the consequences. His ashes were scattered over the airfield.

There existed a healthy but unofficial rivalry between the three squadrons based at Hornchurch. Nos 54 and 65 Squadrons tipped the scales slightly as they were flying Gloster Gladiators. The Gladiator was faster and overall a better performer than the Gauntlet with a speed of 253 mph. In any case, they easily outclassed the beaten up old Gauntlets No. 74 were flying at the time.

'We could all fly aeroplanes and we could fly them well but unfortunately 74 Squadron was equipped with Gauntlets which had been in countless numbers of Squadrons before they were eventually pushed on to 74. When it was serviceable it was a lovely aeroplane'.

When it was unserviceable it was a miserable experience as John would soon find out. 'Freeborn ...', Treacy called out in his Irish accent, '... You can fly home this weekend. That's if you can find your bloody way to Leeds, wherever Leeds may be!' Treacy sarcastically retorted. 'I was very surprised ...' John recalls '... and so I excitedly began to plan my route home to Headingly'. After planning his journey out and flying home for the weekend in a tired old Gauntlet, John subsequently spent the whole of Sunday 'Waiting for the damn thing to be fixed'.

Aside from this one unfortunate occurrence, John's flights back to the North were generally a joyous time. 'I enjoyed the trips home because I would meet a lot of my old school chums in Headingly and when they found out I was a pilot flying a single-seater fighter, the pints went down my throat until I was so drunk I didn't know where I was. But most of all I had a lot of pleasure observing the reaction of my old school masters when they saw ''Bad boy John Freeborn'' flying an aeroplane'.

John remembers one particular occasion at home with fondness. It was the time he met up with his old Physical Training teacher, Mason Clark in a local pub. Mason was possibly the only teacher John ever liked and so when he asked John if he would fly over the school on his return to Hornchurch, the Pilot Officer gladly obliged. On the morning of his return John flew over the school and landed his aircraft down on the green grass of the cricket pitch at the front of the school and taxied around to see young boys cheering. Although he couldn't hear them over his noisy engine, the sight of those boys waving their arms at him filled him with elation as he prepared to take off again. 'I hoped that nobody else had seen me land because I would have been in for some trouble, but nobody did and when I got back to Hornchurch, all was well'.

It was moments like this that gave John appreciation for their beat-up old Gauntlets, not to mention the weekly 30,000 foot battle climb the Squadron would perform. It was exciting and fulfilling for the young tiger. The sensation went unmatched; that is until February 1939, when the Squadron bid farewell to their weary Gloster Gauntlets and was re-equipped with something far more special ... Supermarine Spitfires.

It was a happy time for No. 74 because 54 and 65 Squadrons would have to wait until March before they received their Spitfires. To John's satisfaction the tables had turned. 'Bob Tuck was a charming man. We were in different squadrons but I always liked him and when we were flying Spitfires, No. 65 were flying Gladiators and I used to look for him in the sky and shoot the hell out of him'.

During their pre-war time at Hornchurch Freeborn and Tuck would often spar in the air, although later in the Mess, neither would admit to being outdone. Nevertheless, all these years later, John continues to remain impressed with Tuck's flying ability.

In January 1939, Flying Officers Malan and Treacy spent several days at Duxford for an instruction course on the Supermarine Spitfire. There was a lot of excitement surrounding this revolutionary aircraft and promises had finally been made to replace the tired Gauntlets stationed at Hornchurch. However more waiting had to be done because the Spitfires needed a couple of technical adjustments and bad weather prevented their collection on several occasions. The first Squadron to be supplied with Spitfires was No. 19 at Duxford, followed soon after by No. 66. When John first saw the Spitfire flying around Hornchurch he was instantly impressed by its performance. 'God what a speed it went round. I thought what a great aeroplane it was and I wondered if we were going to get them'.

Standing next to John, 'Sammy' Sampson looked out across the aerodrome and watched the Spitfire fly off into the distance. 'Did you enjoy that Spitfire?' He asked. 'Yes sir, it was marvellous', John replied. 'Well ...' Sampson said, '... We're getting them'.

The memorable and most cherished day for 74 Squadron was on the 13 February 1939. Flying in from Eastleigh, former CO of No. 74, D.S. 'Brookie' Brooks delivered their first Spitfire MK. 1, with Malan and Treacy flying in Gauntlets as escort. They flew into Hornchurch in formation and landed nicely on the grass runway. The conversion process had finally begun. The two-bladed fixed-pitched propeller wound down to a standstill and the pilots at Hornchurch eagerly began to investigate this wonderful delivery.

The Spitfire MK.1 was armed with eight browning .303 machine guns and powered by a Merlin II engine. Initially the Squadron's code markings were 'JH' but they were later changed to 'ZP' at the outbreak of war. The Spitfire was a beautiful aeroplane that is adored just as much today as it ever was. Many have commented that with its sleek, elegant fuselage and graceful elliptical wings, it is far too lovely a thing to have been used as a war machine. But aside from its unique and state of the art design, fortunately for Britain it was an exceptional fighter plane. The Spitfire MK.1 could climb to approximately 34,400 feet and could reach an impressive speed of 362mph, with a range of 395 miles. Not only was the Spitfire a spectacular sight to behold but also to hear. The Merlin engine had a sound like no other, the kind that stirred confidence in a pilot's heart. With the arrival of No. 74's first Spitfire and the return visit from the popular 'Brookie' Brooks, the Squadron found good cause to celebrate.

As the days passed by more Spitfires began to arrive until the Tigers were fully equipped. John was more than thrilled at the sight of them sitting beautifully on the grass aerodrome at Hornchurch.

Another prominent aeroplane in the RAF's armament at this time was the Hawker Hurricane. It was an excellent gun platform that could take a lot of punishment in battle, but although the Hurricane would prove to play an enormous role in the coming conflicts ahead, John doesn't believe it can be compared to the faster and more manoeuvrable Supermarine Spitfire.

The conversion process from biplane to monoplane took some getting used to. John vividly remembers the first time he sat in the Spitfire. It was a daunting and exciting time, totally different to the Gauntlet. Paddy Treacy leant into the cockpit and began reeling off the different instruments and instructions. Taking the time to let it all sink in was not an option in the Spitfire because they had a tendency to overheat quickly. 'Don't sit there gawping at me, get it off the ground!' Treacy said as he jumped down from the wing. John sat there with the Merlin engine humming away in front of him, trying to remember everything he had been told by Treacy who was now walking away from the aircraft. Instantly John became aware of how bad visibility was on the ground in a Spitfire due to its long, heavy nose blocking the way. John gently began to taxi the Spitfire, moving it from side to side in a weaving motion to see where he was going. He used the brakes very carefully; ever mindful that if rashly applied the Spitfire would tip up onto its nose. Thoughts of Treacy seeing one of their precious new Spitfires with its arse in the air didn't bear thinking about. Stopping crosswind, John made a final cockpit check before letting off the brakes and gently opened the throttle. The Merlin engine gave an unforgettable throaty growl as John accelerated down the grass runway. 'I was off and I thought good grief this is fast. I left the ground and flew right between the hangers because I got my trimming wrong. Instead of going straight I was swinging to the right. I looked down at my air speed indicator and I was doing 180 mph. I'd never been so fast in all my life'.

At 180mph the Spitfire climbed further away from the ground below and away into the vast blue yonder. Treacy's instructions began echoing through John's mind. 'That's the undercarriage lever. Lift it up and then manually pump it to bring the under-carriage up'. John glanced at the lever situated on the right-hand side and quickly realised that he would have to switch hands on the control stick to be able to pump-up the undercarriage. John took the stick with his left hand and began pumping the lever with his right. Trying to keep the left hand steady while pumping with the right was a job in itself! In consequence the Spitfire would bob up and down until the craft of it was mastered. Finally the undercarriage retracted into the Spitfire's beautiful wings as it continued to gain height. Once again, John took the control column with his right hand and settled down. 'In due course of time I got control and had a very enjoyable trip'. Now at altitude, John could fully appreciate this magnificent little aeroplane for what it was. The Spitfire's snug cockpit really made the pilot feel one with the aircraft. John relates the sensation to 'slipping on your overalls'. Flying a Spitfire for the first time was a momentous experience in John's life. As he soared over the lovely English countryside below, he felt totally elated and totally free. He looped, rolled and performed some simple aerobatics in the ever graceful Spitfire. 'The thrill I got from flying a Spitfire at between 10,000 to 15,000 feet, flying in and out of big layers of cumulous, seeing a hole in the clouds and going right through it and up the other side, gave all the pleasure a young man could get out of a flying machine'.

After a tremendous time sweeping through the skies, John decided that he ought to be getting back. He searched below for Hornchurch, turning his concentration to getting the 'kite' safely back onto the ground. On locating the aerodrome, John dipped the Spitfire's nose to lose height before making his approach. With continuous checks on the airspeed indicator, John approached at 90mph and successfully landed on the grass runway. Taxiing back to dispersal required the same method of weaving and going easy on the brakes. John returned without incident, feeling entirely chuffed with the whole experience.

It was not long after the Spitfires arrived that 74 Squadron began working out suitable training and tactics for this highly superior aircraft. Hornchurch became regularly visited by various people of importance. On one particular occasion a group of Army Officers was present while Paddy Treacy gave a fantastic solo flying display in a Spitfire. When coming in to land Treacy forgot to pump down the undercarriage to the locked position. Therefore after a fine landing the wheels began to retract into the wings causing the Spitfire to slowly sink into the grass. Funnily enough, one of the army spectators thought it was all part of the performance and complimented the 'manoeuvre'.

On 10 July 1939, John flew to Le Bourget, Paris with the Squadron to celebrate the Fall of Bastille with the French Air Force until 14 July. Previously, when John had been serving as the Squadron Adjutant, he was sworn to secrecy as maps of France and information regarding the Squadron's invitation started rolling in. 'I was completely surrounded by members of the squadron who would ask: "What are those maps that have come in?". "Nothing to do with you lot". "Oh yes it is, we want to know. Grab him!" And I thought, "Oh no, into the emergency water tank I go again", but I managed to get away from them. Until later: "What are they?" "They're only maps of Southern England. What do you want with them?" "No they're not". Oh, they called me a liar, a creep, Sampson's running dog and all sorts. A few days later the invitation had been made official and so I was able to release the maps. "We don't want your bloody maps", they said, "We've already got them". And of course, they had picked the lock to the cabinet where the maps were kept'.

John remembers this time as being one of great excitement for him. With the knowledge that he would soon be taking off for Paris, he decided to consult his dear friend Ernie Mayne. 'Ernie was a Flight Sergeant and the Squadron Training and Safety Officer. He was always telling pilots what to do but they didn't care what a Flight Sergeant had to say. I thought what cruel sods they all were. I always listened to Ernie Mayne and that is why I am alive today. He was a wonderful man that served as bugle boy on HMS *Hood* in the First World War, performing trial runs from Portsmouth to Gibraltar in twenty-four hours. What a great feat that was for the Navy, but we had Ernie now, and what a great feat that was for 74 Squadron. Ernie was always helpful and very kind to us. He shot several Germans down in the course of fighting at Dunkirk and the Battle of Britain until he said, "I'll have to have a posting because I can't cope flying with these young men. When going down at great speed, I pull out but my stomach doesn't!" Ernie was very clever; whatever he had to say was sense. Anyway, he gave me my instructions as usual and said, "Don't take the piss out of the French because they've got no sense of humour".'

Before their trip to Paris began the Squadron was briefed by Station Commander Sampson. 'I remember Sampson telling us what he expected from us: "When we get to Le Bourget we shall circle the aerodrome in tight formation and that means wing-tips overlapping and we shall go down and land in formation, wing-tips overlapping or else!" I thought, "And pump the undercarriage down, swopping hands from the stick, to the pump, to the throttle? You needed six bloody hands to fly these Spitfires.'' Anyway the Squadron responded remarkably well'.

It was indeed a great honour for the Tigers to be invited to Paris. They were the only Spitfire Squadron to attend the celebration which made a lasting impression upon the crowds and not to mention morale. 'We flew over in our Spitfires in impeccable formation, it was quite spectacular. We were literally one aeroplane when we landed. We all touched down, wing-tips overlapping and taxied, following Sampson like a line of young ducklings. After we had landed we were presented to a French General that pinched my bloody cheek and said to Sammy, ''I see you've brought the Squadron mascot with you then''. The rest of the Squadron didn't know what to say and I stood dead still, never turning a hair, looking directly ahead, not opening my mouth and Sampson said, ''No, he's one of my pilots, in fact he's the Squadron Adjutant''. The French General looked at him and said, ''I cannot believe that a little boy like this would be allowed to fly a Spitfire. You are funny people, you English''. And so he went on'.

Other than that one awkward experience in Paris, John's boyish looks also came in handy from time to time. One unsuspecting day at Hornchurch, trouble arrived on Sampson's doorstep. Margaret, the girl John had lied to about being dead had finally caught up with him. She arrived at the station with her irate parents. 'Freeborn . . .' Sampson said to John after listening to his dilemma, '. . . I don't want to see you anywhere on this camp today, get lost!' John quickly made his exit just in time. Later in the afternoon, Margaret's parents stormed in to see Sampson protesting that that cheat, that liar, that rotter John Freeborn had to take some responsibility for his actions. 'He is going to marry my daughter whether he likes it or not!' the father declared to Sampson. 'I don't think he'd like that sir', Sammy replied. 'What's it got to do with you!?' the mother retorted. Sampson composed himself before calmly responding. 'I'm his Commanding Officer and you can't do anything because he's a juvenile!' 'What do you mean?' asked the father looking puzzled. 'Well, he's only eighteen and there's nothing you can do until he becomes of age',

Sampson concluded. With nothing left to say the disappointed girl and her parents left Hornchurch without further ado. However, John later said that, 'I was always very sorry to upset her, Margaret was a lovely girl'.

Speaking of his first night in Paris during the celebrations John recalls:

> We were looked after by the French very well. In the evening the Champagne came out and although it wasn't for Pilot Officers I thought 'Sampson won't mind' so I had a glass and after several more I got as drunk as a Billy goat. I went back to my bedroom, laid down and thought 'God, I'm dead. You've done this to yourself you silly sod'. The next day at the hotel I felt horribly hung over and cringed as Sampson announced after breakfast that we would be heading for our Spitfires. Standing in front of us pilots Sampson said: 'We are now going to do a mass flypast from Paris with the French air force and you know how I want you to fly. Take off as a squadron, land as a squadron, wing-tips overlapping and I'll be watching'. I never felt so ill in all my life from the night before but somehow with my hands going all over the place and a throbbing head, I managed to carry on as I was expected to do. When we landed the French pilots cheered us and I remember thinking how wonderful that was. They invited us into their hanger for a drink and I have never known anything to work so well for a hangover than their cheap and nasty beer. It cleared my head immediately.

Shortly after, the Squadron were told that they would be going to the British Embassy that evening to meet the Ambassador. The boys of 74 looked very smart that evening dressed in tails and white ties. When John walked into the embassy he got the shock of his life at the palatial interior. 'It made any RAF station look like a dump. In we went where we met the Ambassador and his wife, then we shook hands with his lackeys and hoped they'd put some drink our way'.

With no drink forth coming, the boys took some initiative. They soon discovered that there was a crate of beer behind the band that was playing in the embassy. Being the only Pilot Officer in sight, the job of retrieving the beer fell to John. Very cautiously John began to make his way around the band and towards the beer. 'As I was taking the beer out of the crate there was a hand the size of a gorilla's that grabbed my arm. It was one of the band's guardsman. He held my arm so tight I thought it was going to break, so I slipped the beer back into the crate and apologised for assuming it was ours'. Disappointed by his efforts, Flying Officer Mainwaring turned to John. 'Are we going to stay here?' he asked. John looked towards the busy entrance of the embassy. 'How the hell can we get out the front door with all those service police officers there?' 'No, we don't go that way', Mainwaring said, 'We go over the bloody railings'. 'So there we were in tails climbing over the rails of the British Embassy and off we went to Montmartre where we had a cracking night I tell you.' The following morning Mainwaring and Freeborn got a call from Sampson. 'Where did you get to last night?' Sampson enquired. 'Oh, we were around, enjoying ourselves at the embassy', John replied trying his best to sound convincing. 'You know bloody well you didn't', Sampson remarked, 'So, come on, where did you go?' 'We went to Montmartre sir'. 'How on earth did you get there?' Sampson asked looking surprised. 'We had to climb the railings sir.' The two pilots stood still for a moment and braced themselves for a rollicking. 'Good show lads, I'm glad you did it, glad you enjoyed yourselves', Sampson said as he walked away. Later John reflected that 'You never knew with Sampson!' John's final memory of his time in Paris is when the Squadron was packing up to leave. 'The Spitfire had two flare chutes you see. So at night time you could drop the flares and hopefully see the enemy but they weren't good for that, what they were good for was stashing champagne bottles in. We all filled our aircraft with bottles and back to Hornchurch we went'. When the boys arrived back at the aerodrome they were unhappily greeted by customs officers who carried out thorough searches all over their aircraft. 'They didn't find anything until some fool of a man opened a chute on one of the Spitfires and a bottle of Champagne fell onto the tarmac and burst. Oh we did have some trouble with those awful customs people'.

A few days after 74 Squadron's return from France, some new faces began to appear around the station. In August commander-in-chief Hugh Dowding's son, Pilot Officer Derek Hugh Dowding also joined the Tigers ranks. It was not long after his arrival that tragedy struck the Squadron when a new recruit, Sergeant Gower, was killed in a flying accident.

In this same month, 74 Squadron was again involved with the French Air Force in a Home Defence Exercise. The French came across the Thames Estuary to 'mock bomb' London in their weary, outdated aircraft. No. 74 Squadron dived down with their neighbouring squadrons to intercept them. The French-men left their tight formations, scattering in all directions. John remembers seeing aircraft everywhere. 'We scared the living daylights out of them! We got so close. It was the most frightening flight I ever had in a Spitfire. I was flying as Red Two, Malan was Red One and we dived down on this bomber formation. My air speed indicator was somewhere in the region of 400mph. We were going like the clappers towards them and then Malan rapidly pulled out and shot back up into the sky. I was going too quickly to follow him and I went right through the formation of bombers. I was so close I could see the pilots. How I didn't hit one I don't know'.

Over the following weeks and months 74 Squadron was kept extremely busy by their Flight Commanders Treacy and Malan who were adamant on preparing their young men for what surely lay ahead. Not only were the pilots kept active during this pre-war time but also the Squadron's ground crew. Derrick Morris, one of 74 Squadron's armourers remembers the time well:

In 1939, I was an airman and John was a Pilot Officer. A P.O. may be the lowest commissioned rank but an airman approached officers with caution! I remember John as one of the pilots who spent most of their time in the crew room at the front of our hanger. Those pilots who I had conversations with and I remember most are; Flying Officer 'Tinky'

Measures and both Flight Commanders, Malan and Treacy. When I arrived Flight Sergeant Gardener was in charge of the armament section – who I rarely saw!

In each flight there were about six or seven armourers doing daily inspections and routine gun cleaning or in the hanger doing periodic inspections (which was 30 hours flying time and later in 1940 it increased to 40 hours) and major gun repairs. Two of us dealt with a steady stream of 30, 60, 90 and 120 hour inspections which involved the armament tank being removed of all guns for examination and repairs, their replacements, harmonisations and butt testing. We were also responsible for the gun sight, camera gun and the pneumatic gun firing system. Once the guns were reinstalled we handled the Spitfires out to the tarmac between the hangers and jacked the aircraft up and using spirit levels got the aircraft into flying position exactly 50 yards from the painted pattern of spots on the hanger door. Once the guns, gun sight and camera gun were adjusted to bear on the appropriate spots we were required to have it checked by a pilot before we wire locked the gun mountings in position. I used to poke my head around the pilot's crew room door and ask for someone to come and check; more often than not I got one of the Sergeant Pilots for the job. Subsequently we pushed the Spitfire round to the stop butts, jacked the tail up and fired the guns. We had short belts of about 15 rounds in each ammo tank. Hopefully there would be no stoppages! The discussions with 'Maxie' Malan and Paddy Treacy were usually about the harmonisation, Malan in particular got us to make a harmonisation spot on a wooden pole, and for his Spitfire we levelled the aircraft pointing towards the airfield. We would then get a volunteer to take the pole a measured 250 yards out on the grass. All guns, gun sight and camera gun were then adjusted to that spot. The .303 bullet had a flat trajectory up to that range then the bullet drop started when gravity began to affect the flight of the bullet. Malan was always known to us at that time as 'Maxie' and Treacy was 'Paddy' although his family always called him 'Patsy'. The first mention of 'Sailor' Malan that I knew of was when his name was mentioned in newspapers after I had left the squadron. They were a pair of nice men and the two of them really ran the Squadron as we rarely saw the CO. They saw to training and practice of their pilots and were both well thought of.

For the fighter pilots of 74 Squadron, the time was fast approaching where mock dogfights and friendly interceptions would become a thing of the past. In the coming months ahead, dogfights would be fiercely fought with live ammunition and interceptions would be a matter of life and death for the civilians helplessly watching from below the heavens. The RAF still remained vastly outnumbered in comparison to Göring's mighty *Luftwaffe*. By the summer of 1939, the *Luftwaffe's* strength approached 4,000 aircraft, 1,100 of which was the Messerschmitt Bf 109 single-engine fighter. During the Battle of Britain, the RAF was outnumbered by four to one.

The 1 September 1939, became a cataclysmic day for the world but particularly for the ill prepared Polish people. German armed forces invaded Poland on Hitler's insubstantial pretext that Germany had to retaliate due to Polish border violations. The Polish defences were spread abysmally thin along the borders which caused little obstruction for the war hungry attackers. The German army attacked from the north, south and west, swiftly pushing the Polish army to the east. The spearhead of the invasion was conducted by the already battle-hardened *Luftwaffe*, the sharp point being the Ju 87 Stuka dive bombers along with other *Luftwaffe* bombers such as He 111s and Do 17s which effectively attacked airfields, railway junctions, bridges and strategic roads. The ill-equipped Polish Air Force stood little chance with their limited and antiquated aircraft. The poorly armoured PZL P.11 Polish fighter planes had an ineffectual rate of climb and could barely reach 200mph. In consequence the Polish fighters could not adequately reach the German bombers to intercept them which had devastating effects on ground forces and civilians.

The first generally accepted air victory claimed in World War II took place within the first week of heavy fighting when a Ju 87 pilot at Cracow shot down a P.11c taking off. Notwithstanding the inferior aircraft the Poles were flying, they fought with inspiring might, claiming 134 air victories, but ultimately to no avail. With approximately 400 aircraft the Polish held little hope against the *Luftwaffe*'s strength of over 2,000. As well as being outnumbered the Polish army also lacked motorised transport which was hugely debilitating because they were forced to rely on foot infantry and horse-drawn transport. With an overwhelming amount of German soldiers and Panzer divisions surrounding them, Poland rapidly collapsed. A new and frightening word began to roll like thunder across the British shores – *Blitzkrieg*.

The 3 September 1939, was a Sunday. The weather that morning was bright and sunny in the South of England; it seemed like an inappropriate backdrop considering the news that would soon arrive. At 10 am the wireless spoke across the whole of Britain: 'Stand by for an announcement of national importance.' Everyone at Hornchurch sat or stood around feeling impatient and edgy. It wasn't as if they didn't know what was coming but somehow waiting for it seemed worse. John was waiting in the dining room at the time with his fellow Squadron members. Not only would the news determine the country's immediate future but it would also select the winner of the Squadron's betting pool! Finally the tension was broken at 11:15 am when the Prime Minister's voice came over the airwaves. The tired, almost inconsolable voice of Neville Chamberlain spoke:

> *I am speaking to you from the Cabinet room at 10 Downing Street. This morning the British Ambassador in Berlin handed the German Government a final note stating that unless we heard from them by eleven o'clock that they were prepared at once to withdraw their troops from Poland, a state of war would exist between us. I have to tell you that no such undertaking has been received and that consequently this country is at war with Germany.*

The announcement left a subdued taste in John's mouth. He wasn't afraid or apprehensive, neither was he excited. A job was now at hand and he would see it through. As for the betting pool 'The bloody chef won it'.

A great urgency swept over Hornchurch following Neville Chamberlain's broadcast. The Mess was vacated and personnel moved into tents and trailer caravans by the aircraft. The following days were spent filling sandbags and constructing blast-proof dispersals for the Spitfires. John remembers this unified effort at Hornchurch well. The early hours of the morning at dispersal took some getting used to, but John and his Flight Commander made use of their time together.

> In the early mornings I would walk up and down the perimeter track with my good friend at the time, Sailor Malan. We used to talk about all sorts of things, including our lives. I think I knew more about Malan back then than anyone. We were very close despite the fact he was my Flight Commander and later my Squadron Commander.

In the early morning hours of 4 September, the eerie wail of air raid sirens sounded. Scotland Yard had received a telephone call from a man in Guildford claiming to have spotted a large formation of bombers flying over the town. At 0250 hours, 74 Squadron's 'A' Flight was ordered to scramble. Flying Officer Measures and Sergeant Hawkins took off with Flight Lieutenant Malan leading Red Section. Shortly after, Yellow Section received instructions to follow the pursuit. Flying Officer Byrne lifted off from the dark airfield, accompanied by Sergeant Flinders and Pilot Officer Freeborn flying Spitfire K9865. They were given orders to patrol by sections to intercept an enemy raid supposedly approaching from the coast of Holland. After a little more than an hour of searching the empty skies with wide eyes and pounding hearts, the pilots landed their Spitfires in frustration. The mystery formation of aircraft was later identified as friendly bombers returning via Felixstowe.

It was around this time that some new faces began to appear around Hornchurch. John was delighted to see that they were generally around his own age. One morning in early September John looked up from his office desk to see a tall, slender and charming looking Pilot Officer standing in the doorway. The young man gave a magnificent salute and said: 'My name is John Mungo Park sir, and I've been posted to 74 Squadron'. 'You don't call me sir ...' John said, '... I'm only the Adjutant!' John introduced himself to the new recruit and the two pilots firmly shook hands. 'I'm glad to meet you John', Mungo said in his Liverpudlian accent. And this was the start of a great friendship that never ended until John left the Squadron.

As ever, Malan and Treacy kept the Squadron busy with their training and in addition John continued to learn from the wise 39 year old, Ernie Mayne, who advised him to practice his manoeuvres and aerobatics as much as he possibly could. John recalls one occasion that didn't go according to plan. At around 4,000 feet, John prepared himself for a practice forced landing. When he closed the throttle to glide in to the aerodrome, a warning horn sounded in the cockpit to alert him that his under-carriage was retracted.

> *I switched it off because it was blasting through my earphones and blowing my head off. The red light on the dashboard was flashing because my undercarriage wasn't down and so I switched all the precautions off because I thought it would be easier to do this without all the distraction.*

When John made his final approach to the aerodrome, he had forgotten all about his undercarriage and foolishly landed on his belly. In consequence a Court of Enquiry was conducted. John was severely reprimanded for the error and was duly brought before Sir Hugh Dowding. As a result of his mishap, John was fined £5 but Sir Hugh Dowding, ever aware of a pilot's wages, paid the fine out of his own pocket. 'It was a silly thing to do wasn't it?' Dowding remarked from his desk. 'Yes sir', Pilot Officer Freeborn replied. 'Right, get out of my office! I don't want to see you again'. 'That was the kind of man Lord Dowding was. A superb commander, clever and kind in his ways, as you have no doubt seen in the many occasions he talked about his fighter boys, as though he was a father to us all'.

Commenting on this unfortunate incident John is reminded that the whole affair could have been avoided by the actions of a pilot from North Weald who was down on the aerodrome at the time, watching him come in with his wheels fully up. 'There was a Hurricane that could have taxied in front of me, which would have made me go round again and open the throttle. All the actuators would have come in telling me the undercarriage was down'. John later discovered that the Hurricane pilot was Squadron Leader Donaldson from 151 Squadron, who apparently wanted to see what would happen. John was not impressed. In due course the Air Ministry sent John a letter to further condemn his hapless landing. John framed it in a toilet seat.

Illustration by David Pritchard

CHAPTER THREE

Barking Creek

The declaration of war spread like wildfire across the country. Peacetime had suddenly disappeared like a passing cloud, leaving the British awfully tense and jumpy. The air raid sirens had already bellowed several times without justification, but now terrible thoughts began to accumulate in peoples minds. Now that England was at war with Germany, surely the Capital would be attacked in great force and with all manner of terror weapons? Dark fears of poisonous gasses being dropped, germ warfare and exploding houses antagonized the nation like a deadly plague. It is little wonder the RAF sat on edge with an inexorable determination to protect its homeland. The *Luftwaffe's* bombs were imminent and the responsibility for stopping them belonged to eager young fighter boys like John Freeborn.

In the early hours of the morning, a low mist crept across the airfield at North Weald on Wednesday 6 September 1939. The serene aerodrome barely stirred as chirping birds stretched their wings across the flight path, gliding over the Hurricanes dozing peacefully in the morning dew. At approximately 0615 hours, the silence was shattered when the Sector Operations' telephone rang. The message was loud and clear. Searchlight batteries had reported aircraft flying in the vicinity of West Mersea, Essex. Three minutes later, Sector Operations at North Weald contacted

45

HQ, No. 18 Group, Observer Corps, with the information it had
received from the batteries reports. At 0627 North Weald contacted them a second time, announcing they had scrambled six
fighters from 56 Squadron in an easterly direction. (However,
the official operations book for 56 Squadron states that they were
brought to readiness at 0630 and airborne at 0640. Whatever the
exact time was does nothing to dispel the fact that a disastrous
error in judgement was made.) HQ had only authorised one
Flight (six aircraft) to be ordered off but instead the Squadron's
Commanding Officer scrambled the entire unit.

One by one, aircraft raced across the airfield intent on finding
the ever nearing Hun. As the Hurricanes leapt into their natural
element, the pilots desperately began to climb, with their rotating
props cutting the cool September air. As the Squadron formed up
over North Weald, two young pilots watched from below, toying
with the idea of joining them. After getting into formation, the
twelve Hurricanes set off for their patrol line of 11,000ft between
Harwich and Colchester. On making their decision, the two pilots
left behind, rashly took off in reserve aircraft and flew after their
Squadron. They eventually caught up with them over the coast
and continued to fly about half a mile behind and 1,000ft below
the main group of Hurricanes. The leading formation remained
totally unaware of their presence. Back at North Weald, the
Controller of Sector Operations, Group Captain D.F. Lucking
discovered that a full Squadron was now airborne instead of just
one Flight. Lucking made a terrible mistake and failed to recall
the unauthorised aircraft, which would later have devastating
consequences.

By now, the shrill sound of the air raid sirens wailed across
the south-east of Essex. Twenty raids had been plotted by RDF
(Radar) and taken from sources in the Observer Corps, plus an
additional number of fifty hostile aircraft reported near Southend
by No. 11 Group. It was more than likely that a German attack
would be expected to come from the south-easterly section of
England, so with the large formation of aircraft in this particular
zone, the signs pointed to a mass attack on London. To counteract the threat, Hurricanes of 151 Squadron stationed at North
Weald were scrambled. They quickly left the dew covered grass

of the aerodrome and climbed in the direction of the rising sun with Squadron Leader E.M. Donaldson leading.

As the fog swept across Hornchurch aerodrome, John Freeborn with his fellow pilots of 74 Squadron waited at dispersal full of apprehension and wonder until suddenly they were relieved from the torment of readiness and 'A' Flight was scrambled into action. Dashing towards his trusty steed, John's heart pounded with anxiety and excitement at the thought of finally being able to put his training into use. Leaping up onto the port wing then settling down into the snug cockpit, the young man strapped himself in and began to prepare for take-off. First to leave the airfield was Sailor Malan leading Red Section at approximately 0645 hours. Yellow section was soon to follow but was slightly delayed due to a problem with Yellow leader Paddy Byrne's engine. Several moments thereafter, Yellow Section was airborne with John Freeborn flying as Yellow 2 and Sergeant Pilot 'Polly' Flinders as Yellow 3. 'I could see Malan once we got airborne, quite a few miles ahead on his way to the point where the enemy supposedly were. In actual fact, when Malan got there it was an Anson of Coastal Command'.

Climbing to their vectored height the two sections finally joined up and cast their eyes around the vast blue arena before them, vigorously searching for the enemy. The tension was so thick John could taste it as he stayed in tight formation whilst scanning the hostile skies with fervent concentration. Suddenly the search was over. Sailor Malan called, 'Tally-Ho! Number One attack-Go!' over the radio and Yellow Section plunged into action. Catching sight of a wide, loose 'vic' formation (the type of formation believed to be advocated by the enemy) John followed Paddy Byrne into a dive heading for the formation below. With the heat of battle burning as brightly as the morning sun, not to mention the sheer speed of aerial combat, the Spitfire pilots of 74 were unable to make a clear identification of the main formation but pressed on to attack two aircraft thought to be Messerschmitt 109s flying behind and slightly below. Byrne and Freeborn swept into the attack and fired at the two fighters, thought to be German fighter escort. Seeing the action from the cockpit of his Hurricane, Squadron Leader Donaldson of 151 Squadron was left to watch on in horror as a tragedy unfolded before his eyes. Relating this particular incident many years later, Donaldson remarks:[1]

> I saw two of the Spitfires turn in on two of the Hurricanes and open fire. I yelled over the R/T. 'Do not retaliate. They are friendly!' A frantic melee ensued, but not one of the North Weald wing fired, although there was a frantic manoeuvring by almost everyone.

Unbeknown to Byrne and Freeborn they were successfully attacking two Hurricanes of 56 Squadron, flown by Pilot Officers M.L. Hulton-Harrop and F.C. Rose, the same two pilots who had rashly decided to take off in reserve aircraft and follow their Squadron from North Weald into action.

Donaldson continues:

> The targeted Hurricanes were split up. Hulton-Harrop must have been hit by gunfire for his aircraft did not seem to be damaged substantially. It glided down in a left turn until it struck the ground apparently quite gently.
>
> I managed to get the wing re-formed and we landed back at North Weald very angry at the terrible mess-up where our controllers had so irresponsibly vectored two wings onto each other, guns loaded and pilots warned for combat.

Upon landing Donaldson was informed by his mechanic that Air Vice-Marshall Keith Park, AOC of 11 Group, had sacked Group Captain Lucking and had sent for him to be brought back to Group Headquarters. (However it is worth mentioning that once the ordeal had settled, Lucking was soon reinstated.)

The costly errors made that day had tragically taken the life of Hulton-Harrop. Later reports claimed that Hulton-Harrop had been hit by gun-fire to the back of the head, becoming the first British pilot casualty of WWII. Pilot Officer Rose narrowly survived the attack after force landing his damaged aircraft in a sugar-beet field.

[1] *The Blitz: Then and Now*, Winston G. Ramsey 1990

Utterly unaware of the severity of their situation, Yellow Section peeled away feeling elated with their success, after all, in their minds, they had just shot down the Hun, exactly as they had been trained to do. On heading back to base Freeborn lost track of Byrne but soon caught sight of a Blenheim which he mistook for an invader.

> I saw another aircraft that I thought was an 88, so I went after it until Sergeant 'Polly' Flinders, flying as Yellow 3, swiftly manoeuvred between me and the 'enemy'. I cursed him on the radio, 'Get out the way, I saw it first', I said. 'You can't shoot it, it's a Blenheim!' I then realised that it was a Blenheim and not an 88. Flinders being the nice, kindly guy he was, got in the way and saved their lives.

The incident now known as 'The Battle of Barking Creek' was made top secret at the time and discussions concerning the matter were strictly forbidden. The 6 September 1939, that dreadful Wednesday, would forever stay in John's mind.

As Pilot Officer Freeborn touched down on the grassy airfield at Hornchurch and taxied into dispersal he was immediately placed under close arrest. One can't even imagine the awful emotions that filled the pit of nineteen year old John Freeborn's stomach from being told he was under arrest for shooting down a friendly aircraft. As he sat in a secluded room looking at Johnny Allen who had been placed on the door as his guard, John's thoughts began to race as fast as the incident itself. Despite feeling an unquenchable guilt for his actions he was certain that his career as an RAF fighter pilot was over. The silence was deafening, the wait even worse. He couldn't understand what had happened, what had gone wrong. He was positive that Flight Commander Malan had called, 'Tally-Ho! Number One attack-Go!' over the R/T; and positive that he had followed the instruction. The agony would continue for the distraught Pilot Officer and in many ways it still does. At the same time Paddy Byrne was also being held under close arrest and Sailor Malan, having already landed was nowhere to be seen. However he was later thoroughly debriefed by Sammy Sampson. John remembers the events that day:

> We landed at Hornchurch and there was Sampson. I thought 'Oh, he's coming to see us land. I'm going to get a pat on the back from my great chum and CO'. But it wasn't forth coming, I was sent to my room under close arrest, Byrne was sent to his room under close arrest, and at no time were we allowed to communicate. Then I heard Sampson shouting at the top of his voice 'Where is Malan? I want him here now!' and someone said, 'Malan's gone home'. He lived with his wife out of Hornchurch and did his usual bunk. Anybody could be in trouble but him. Anyway, he was sent for.
> I was in my room when there was a knock at the door and Johnny Allen from 54 Squadron came in and said 'I'm your guard. You're not allowed out, you're not allowed to speak to anyone and you're not allowed any visitors. I am totally in charge of you'. The same thing happened with Byrne and his guard was a member of 65 Squadron. We weren't allowed to use the telephone, we weren't allowed to do anything. Whilst I was there sitting in a room wondering what was going to happen to me, frightened to death, being only a kid, I thought something has got to happen ... and it did. Sampson came to see me and asked about the incident. He kicked Johnny Allen out and said, 'Now we'll talk together about what happened because you are in serious trouble'. And I realised I was. I had done what I should not have done. Being the Squadron Adjutant I had taken the pilots' squadron order book around and got everybody to sign it under the condition that we would not, under any circumstances, attack a single-engine aircraft and here I was, the bloke that had carried the book around, got all the signatures and I was a culprit, I had shot a single-engine aircraft down.

Referring to the engagement, John continues:

> We got right on top of them and it turned out to be two Hurricanes which we immediately shot down, despite the fact

that it said in our pilots' order books that we weren't to attack single-engine aircraft or anything of this nature. Malan gave the order to attack and attack we did. Had we not done what he had told us, no doubt we would have been in desperate trouble for not doing it. I know that I shot one down and it was a very sad thing when I found out it was a pilot who had jumped out of bed, still in his pyjamas, got into a Hurricane and chased the rest of the squadron without permission from anyone.

John recalls how helpful Sammy Sampson was during this difficult time for the frightened pilot. He did his best to aid both Freeborn and Byrne, who now faced a court martial at Fighter Command Head Quarters. Given the serious nature of the situation, John was shocked to witness Paddy's laidback attitude towards their plight. While they were under close arrest John remembers receiving messages from the Irishman joking that at least now they could join the Air Transport Auxiliary and that it was 'better pay anyway.' The Yorkshireman was never able to understand Byrne's attitude during that period and even though they were seemingly in the same boat John felt absolutely alone.

Time went on and we had the Court of Enquiry that was ordered by Keith Park. There was nothing nice about it. It was held in camera and of course nobody knew anything about it, particularly my old friend Sammy Hoare who has had so much to say about the 'Battle of Barking Creek', when he knew absolutely nothing about it at all. Many people have put their views forward, many of them totally wrong because they just did not know what had happened.

The whole ordeal had evolved from a series of mistakes and faulty radar equipment. One Blenheim that was wrongly identified by the Observer Corps had somehow, through terrible communication failures, transpired into a whole squadron of 'enemy bombers.' The consequence of such assumptions led to two Hurricane pilots being shot down and two Spitfire pilots being placed under arrest.

In due course George Sampson changed the bonds of close arrest to open arrest. 'That meant I couldn't go into the Mess, I couldn't talk to the other pilots of our three squadrons there, but I could go out'.

After taking onboard Sampson's advice to visit Bentley Priory, John sought out an Intelligence Officer at Fighter Command Headquarters by the name of Sir Patrick Hastings. Hastings was an excellent Barrister who was well regarded in his time. He readily accepted John's request to defend him in Court and then sent him off to Biggin Hill where he was to ask Roger Bushell to work as his number two on the case. Roger Bushell, a man famed today for his legendary part in 'The Great Escape' before he was coldly murdered by the Gestapo, was at this time the Commanding Officer of 601 Squadron stationed at Biggin Hill. When John explained his situation to Bushell he contacted Hastings and accepted the responsibility.

The hearing was held at Bentley Priory on 17 October 1939. John sat nervously with Paddy Byrne but felt confident in the two men defending them. The prosecutor was an RAF lawyer and the Judge Advocate was a man named Sterling. John took an instant dislike to Sterling and felt uncomfortable with the knowledge that Sterling had previously only served as clerk to the court, but he had no say in the matter at hand.

In addition there were four tribunal officers that consisted of an Air Vice Marshal, an Air Commodore and two Group Captains. The hearing lasted several hours until the verdict ended proceedings. Pilot Officer John Freeborn and Flying Officer Vincent Byrne were rightly acquitted of the incident.

Being completely exonerated was a huge relief for the young pilot and Roger Bushell's words, 'Don't worry John, you're all clear, it's all over' became a soothing declaration to the young Freeborn. Naturally the traumatic experience of Barking Creek would always remain with John as would his total distain for Adolph Malan.

At Bentley Priory Malan had appeared for the prosecution stating that he had given a second order to break off from the attack once he had realised that they were friendly aircraft but neither Freeborn nor Byrne heard the alleged instruction.

John was thoroughly hurt that Malan had appeared for the prosecution instead of the defence and could not have agreed more when Hastings called Malan 'A bare faced liar!' in court. John states:

> *The sad part about it was that Malan gave evidence for the prosecutors. Malan stood there and lied his heart out about what he'd done and what he'd said in telling us not to fire, that they were British and we should have known it. But nobody heard it. Nobody heard him say a word on the radio, not even his dear friend Sergeant Hawkins. In fact the dislike of Hawkins from the Court was such that they wouldn't have him in.*

Feeling disappointed and betrayed by his Flight Commander an obvious rift divided both Tigers leaving John extremely angry towards Malan's conduct. John feels that Malan was only watching out for himself and ever since that day John has never been able to forget it and neither it seemed did Malan. John is convinced that because of the outcome of the Barking Creek episode, Malan was solely responsible for halting John's progression in the Squadron and despite Freeborn's achievements he never recommended him for any awards, which were surely deserved. 'My association with Malan came to an end. I never spoke to him unless I had to and he only spoke to me when he wanted something doing'.

From the court hearing onwards, wherever Malan was socially, John was not, but in the skies John was able to maintain his professionalism and respect for Malan as a fighter pilot, leader and tactician. Although walks around the aerodrome together became a thing of the past, Malan would often run ideas by John when it concerned the Squadron. Both John and Malan were well aware that with the coming months ahead it was essential that they put their differences aside and focused on the gruelling task before them.

Illustration by David Pritchard

CHAPTER FOUR

Dunkirk

I n October 1939, the Squadron began using Rochford aero-drome as their forward base. It was here that formation practice, air gunnery training and night flying was conducted but the following months seemed uneventful and painstakingly dull. The 'Phoney War' as it is known was a frustrating time for John as he remembers living in tents close to their aircraft and being on alert for raids that never developed. It was a time of idleness, waiting around for something to happen and basically sheer boredom for the boys of 74 Squadron.

On 22 October, Paddy Byrne left the Tigers and was posted into 92 Squadron stationed at Biggin Hill. No. 92 Squadron's Commanding Officer at this time was Roger Bushell and Byrne was immediately attached to 601 Squadron for a conversion course on Blenheims. John had thought he'd seen the last of the Irishman but on 4 May 1940, Paddy Byrne turned up in the Adjutant's office. 'What are you doing back?' John asked. 'I've been posted back to 74 Squadron', Byrne replied, much to John's displeasure.

During the long weeks of the 'Phoney War' the Tigers began to fly convoy patrols from Dover to Calais, escorting the ships below and sweeping the skies for hostile aircraft. However due to the lack of aerial activity at this time, the pilots kept busy by entertaining themselves and the sailors down below with aerobatics. John clearly remembers one occasion where he was flying with Malan and Hawkins over the Channel and doing remarkably well to out manoeuvre them.

We'd be escorting a ship from Dover to Calais and Malan, as usual, had to do his showing off bit. So there we were doing formation aerobatics, without Hawkins because he could never keep up. When the ship had docked at Calais we left to come back to Rochford. As we were nearing we were flying very low into the Thames Estuary, so low we were making a wake across the water. I thought 'I wonder how much fuel we've got?' and I pressed the button on the bottom petrol tank and it showed empty. The top tank of course drains into the bottom tank so there was no point in pressing that button. The bottom tank was showing empty, so I called Malan and said, 'Let's go into Manston and refuel'. He said, 'Bloody nonsense, we don't need any fuel'. 'My tank says empty', I said. 'That's because you've been flying like a damn fool and wasting your petrol'. Anyway, he continued on and wouldn't go into Manston so I said, 'If we can't go and get some fuel, can we get some height?' So we climbed up to about 7,000 feet and my engine stopped; I had run out of fuel completely. I was just in between the North Foreland and Rochford and so I called them up and told them I was out of petrol. 'Serves you bloody well right'. They couldn't care less, either of them. So I thought 'Right, you're not going to win this one' and I flew my aircraft so economically that it was unbelievable. I had everything as safe as I could possibly get it. I couldn't do anything with the propeller, it just windmilled, I didn't put the flaps down, didn't pump the undercarriage down, I just kept going gently, literally holding it on the stick. I thought 'As soon as I clear the railway line my undercarriage is going down'. As I was going over countless numbers of telegraph wires, the undercarriage went down and I thought 'You damn fool' because if I had hit the wires I would have gone in, but I cleared them. I touched down very quickly, running faster than I should do, and went right to my dispersal point.

My fitter grabbed the wing tip and swung it round and with the rigger they pushed the Spitfire into the aircraft bay. Then the fitter jumped up onto the wing as he always did, I opened the roof, he dropped the door down and then helped me with the evacuation of the aircraft.

'What have you switched off for sir?' the fitter asked as John climbed out of the cockpit. 'Because I've got no petrol running through', John replied. 'Oh, I wondered why because the other two silly buggers are on the golf course. One's in a bunker, the other's upside down!'

The information was music to John's ears. Hawkins had turned over and Malan had run into a bunker and ended up on his nose. After hearing of John's superb landing, Station Commander 'Daddy' Bouchier approached Malan. 'Freeborn better have an AFC for his flying and putting the aircraft down safely'. 'Just what I was thinking sir!' Malan remarked. 'I'm still waiting for my bloody AFC' John says with a chuckle.

Hair raising experiences in a flying machine like the Spitfire were not uncommon. John recalls another incident which could have ended in disaster.

I was doing an air test with a Spitfire because I would be flying it again at night. All aircraft flying at night had to be air tested in daylight. I came back over Hornchurch at quite a height and I stuck the nose straight down at considerable speed. I tried to pull back on the stick to lose some excess speed but I couldn't pull it back, it was locked solid. I looked down and saw a screwdriver that had dropped down into the universal joints on the bottom of the control column. The only way I could get it out was by going over the vertical, pushing the stick right forward so it dropped out. I rolled out of the inverted position and steadied myself. I was frightened and very annoyed. The poor old fitter that lost his screwdriver was in desperate trouble and rightly so because it was a big shock to me.

In late February John was saddened by the departure of Sammy Sampson who moved on to 10 Group as a Flight Controller.

Sampson had commanded the Squadron with absolute efficiency and had been there for John through some difficult months. His absence was wholly felt around Hornchurch. On 25 February Squadron Leader F.L. White was posted in as supernumerary and on the 1 March he assumed command of the Squadron.

In April the Squadron saw the arrival of Pilot Officers, Harold Gunn, H.M. Stephen, James Young, Arthur Smith and Byron Duckenfield. The latter was to stay but a short while with the Squadron, as Duckenfield explains:

> My time with 74 Squadron was only 24 days: 11 April to 4 May, 1940. This was not a happy time because the CO, Squadron Leader White, took an instant dislike to me. To understand – but not forgive – his attitude, I have to explain the background.
>
> It was Air Ministry Policy at that time (it changed later in the war) to post away immediately from his unit any NCO who was granted a commission. So, I was torn away from the squadron I had flown with for four years. Now, there was an NCO pilot in 74 Squadron, 'Polly' Flinders, who was commissioned on the same date – 1 April – as myself and what happened was this: Flinders was posted from 74 to 32 and I was posted in the other direction, a direct swap. So, this might explain Squadron Leader White's unreasonable resentment: he had lost an experienced fighter pilot and could not accept that he had gained one equally experienced in return. To escape this unhappy atmosphere, I had been in 74 Squadron less than two weeks when I responded to a call for volunteers for the Norwegian campaign. Fortunately for me, tragically for those involved, that campaign failed and I was posted instead to 501 Squadron where, within six days, I was a victim of the Bombay crash at Betheniville. Talk about jumping from the frying pan into fire!

In May 1940, the time for aerobatic displays and convoy patrols had come to an end and life for the Tigers was about to change forever.

Now twenty years of age John Freeborn was once again airborne in hostile skies, flying operational patrols over the channel and off the French coast. To begin with the Squadron was detailed to fly between 6,000 and 7,000 feet but at this altitude they failed to spot any sign of the enemy, so they advanced to a height between 10,000 and 21,000 feet where the sky was much clearer and more effective for finding their adversaries. On 21 May, John along with his companions would meet the enemy for the first time.

In the early evening Sailor Malan led 'A' Flight up above 10/10ths cloud and began to patrol the sky at about 21,000 feet. Flying on Malan's wing-tip as Red Two in Spitfire P8047 was Pilot Officer Freeborn, accompanied by Pilot Officer Bertie Aubert as Red Three. Yellow Section flying nearby consisted of Tink Measures, Pilot Officer Don Cobden and Pilot Officer Ben Draper. Feeling nervous and with tension tingling down his spine, Freeborn held his Spitfire tightly in formation whilst scanning his surroundings for any tell-tale signs of the enemy. As the section passed over the North Foreland John became fully aware of the anti-aircraft fire thumping away to the south-east of their position. As the fighter boys approached Dunkirk in line-astern formation Malan caught sight of two twin-engine aircraft flying a couple of hundred yards apart. After informing the others of the enemy bandits ahead, Malan selected the Heinkel 111 on the right-hand side and lunged into action. Yellow Section broke off for the second bomber. On his first approach Malan overshot the Heinkel which began side-slipping until Malan made a second approach and riddled the bomber with gun-fire at a range of 150 yards closing to about 50. Now only a few hundred feet above cloud the Heinkel made no attempt to duck into it so Malan gave it another long burst and watched his bullets shimmer across the bomber's frame, causing its undercarriage to suddenly drop. Veering off, Freeborn and Aubert followed Malan up and away from the wounded bird and set course towards another formation of enemy aircraft flying roughly 5 miles away from their position. Dropping down into cloud Red Section sped towards their unknowing targets, occasionally surfacing to keep sight of their prey, until finally

three hungry Spitfires reached five Junkers Ju 88s in a clear
opening of white cloud. Gaining ever closer to their prey, Malan
noticed a sixth Ju 88 flying approximately 1,000 yards to the
left of the others. Due to a defective radio the South African
used hand signals that sent Aubert off after the lone bomber
whilst he and Freeborn engaged the main body of aircraft. John
states, 'I was feeling terrible, I didn't know what the matter was
with me. We bumped into some 88s and I followed Malan in'.
Attacking from slightly below and behind at a distance of 200
yards, Freeborn watched as Malan's guns opened up on one of
the Ju 88s. Malan made his second attack from dead astern
which silenced the rear gunner. 'I was right behind Malan. He
put the Ju 88's port engine right out and then its tail burst
into flames. I still felt terrible, I couldn't breathe, I couldn't do
anything. Then I looked down at my instruments and found that
I didn't have my oxygen on! So as soon as I turned it on, I was
back to my old self. I attacked one of the 88s giving it a good long
burst, raking it from nose to tail'. As the Ju 88 fell from the sky
like a heavy stone, John pushed the control column forward and
ducked down into cloud cover feeling elated with his success.

Speaking of the Junkers Ju 88, John remarks:

> *They were difficult to shoot down, but early on in the war
> they hadn't got the tricks off that the other 88 pilots later
> developed. We would get behind them and shoot and they
> would go into a dive. We would be going down at about
> 300mph and all of a sudden the 88s were going past us! What
> had happened? They had put their diving flaps out and air
> brakes on and they would go from 300mph to 100mph just
> like that, and of course there was nothing we could do about
> it until we would go around and come back up to chase them
> again.*

The victorious fighter pilots of 74 Squadron had cause to
celebrate at their performance over Dunkirk that day. Their
first real combat experience was a great confidence builder and
certainly a good morale boost after their bumpy start to the war.

Many pilots carried hidden fears before going into action for the first time. Despite their training the young men worried about how they would handle themselves in a combat situation, thoughts of panic or even cowardice entered their minds like an unwelcomed guest but no one dared admit it. But any fears harboured by the Tigers were now put to rest; they were a Squadron to be reckoned with. On this particular action Freeborn claimed his Ju 88 as a probable but remains sure that he saw it plunging towards the deck, Malan claimed one Ju 88 destroyed and one He 111 as a probable, Measures claimed one He 111 as a probable and Aubert claimed one Ju 88 and one He 111 as a probable.

Initially after their first patrol Bertie Aubert didn't return to Hornchurch until the 23rd because he had to force land near Calais due to low fuel. The American born pilot made it back to base via a Blenheim but a few hours later was lost on another patrol, believed to have been shot down. Not long after Aubert's absence a report came through claiming that a Spitfire was seen being flown by none other than the Germans. Although the circumstances surrounding this claim remain foggy, several of the pilots, including John were of the opinion that it was probably Aubert's aircraft.

By the time John headed off to bed that night he felt exhausted by the whole affair. The next day would be just as taxing.

On 22 May, rubbing the sleep from his eyes, John left his room in the early hours of the morning and made his way down to dispersal. Dawn readiness never got easier.

In some ways the waiting game became more strenuous than the actual fighting. At 0500 hours three sections of Spitfire engines roared into life. With Malan leading, the Squadron climbed away from Rochford and set course for Dover. Forty-five minutes later John would again unleash his guns at the enemy near North Calais. Spotting a Junkers Ju 88 in a clear patch of sky, Malan ordered the Squadron into line astern formation to begin their attack. The Ju 88's crew must have seen the Spitfires coming because the pilot took evasive action and put the Junkers into a steep dive towards the sea below. The Tigers pounced after the bomber, diving at a speed of 400mph.

In order to lose some excess weight the Ju 88 jettisoned four bombs and did its damned best to shake off the fighters but ultimately to no avail. Malan opened the proceedings by firing a couple of short bursts which dealt with the rear gunner. The German pilot put up a hell of a fight as it skidded through the air and turned from side to side getting ever nearer to the deck but Malan continued to blast holes into its fuselage and port engine which caused two streams of white vapour to trail from its engines. As a result Malan's windscreen got covered in glycol engine coolant and so he broke away, leaving Pilot Officer Tony Mould and Freeborn to empty their gun chambers into the bomber. After taking an intense amount of punishment, the Ju 88 proved that it was a formidable adversary but on this occasion it had been defeated. John looked out of his cockpit, watching the Junkers lose height and speed until finally the engines cut out and it dropped down into the cruel sea below. The boys of 74 circled overhead to check for survivors but only an empty dinghy could be seen swaying upon the waves.

The official General Report John made for this engagement reads as follows:

> I was flying as No. 2 of Red section when a Ju 88 was intercepted. The enemy aircraft dived steeply as we approached to attack. He levelled out at 200 feet above the sea and Red Leader delivered a No. 1 attack. White smoke was seen coming out of both motors. Red Leader broke away and Red 3 opened fire at a range of 200 yds. I got one 3 second burst and then the enemy aircraft slowed up suddenly and crashed into the sea. I did not see any rear fire. There were no survivors.

> Signed John Freeborn P/O.

The following day was somewhat quieter for John but not necessarily for some of the chaps stationed at Hornchurch. On a morning patrol 74 Squadron's Commanding Officer, Squadron Leader F.L. White engaged a Henschel 126 with Flying Officer

ilot Officer John Freeborn at the age of 18. (*Tiger Squadron Association*)

Standing left to right: Llewllyn, Stephen, Mungo Park, Draper, Stevenson, Cobden, Smith, Young, Mayne, Hastings. Seated Middle: Malan, White, Measures. Seated front row: Mould, Dowding, Freeborn. (Tiger Squadron Association)

hn Freeborn standing on the wing of Spitfire ZP-C at Manston. (*Tiger Squadron Association*)

anding left to right at Rochford: Don Cobden, Treacy, Mayne, Llewllyn, Mungo Park, Freeborn, ould. Seated left to right: Aubert, White, Dowding (Reading), Measures, Hoare. (*Tiger Squadron ssociation*)

Bob Stanford Tuck. (*Michael Robinson*)

Manston dispersal hut, 1940. Left to right in the doorway: Freeborn, Draper, Franklin. Front row left to right: Mungo Park, St. John. (*Tiger Squadron Association*)

The Tigers at Manston during the Battle of Britain. Left to right: Willie Nelson, Piers Kelly, Peter Stevenson, Don Cobden, Dennis Smith, 'Sailor' Malan, John Mungo Park, John Freeborn, Douglas Hastings, Thomas Kirk, Ernie Mayne, Bill Skinner. (*Tiger Squadron Association*)

The Summer of 1940 at Manston. Left to right: Kirk, Franklin, Richardson, unknown, unknown, Baker (with dog), unknown, Boulding, Szczesny, Malan, unknown, Mungo Park, Draper, unknown, St. John, Skinner, Hilken, Chesters. (*Tiger Squadron Association*)

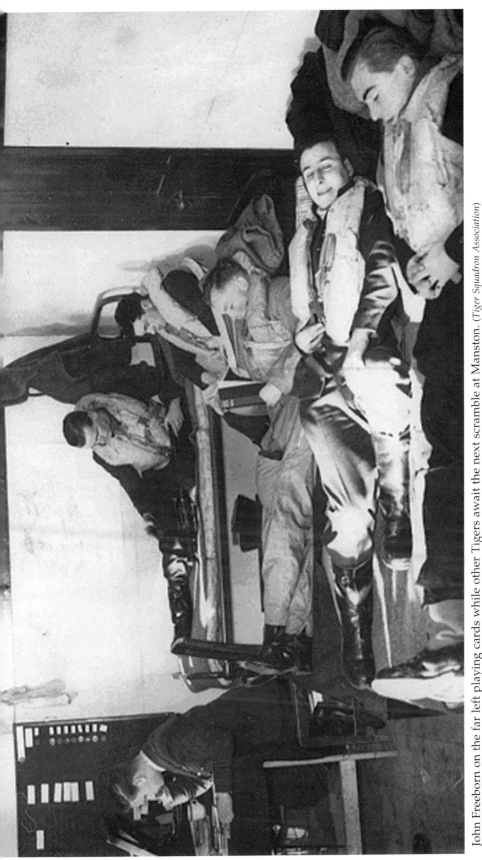

John Freeborn on the far left playing cards while other Tigers await the next scramble at Manston. (*Tiger Squadron Association*)

Vincent 'Paddy' Byrne.
(*Michael Robinson*)

Roger Bushell.
(*Michael Robinson*)

Left to right: Poulton, Freeborn, Wood, Baker and Mould standing by a Spitfire Mk II. (*Tiger Squadron Association*)

Manston, 1940. Boulding, 'Sneezy' Szczesny, H.M. Stephen, Freeborn. (*Tiger Squadron Association*)

John Freeborn and John Mungo Park resting at Wittering. (*Tiger Squadron Association*)

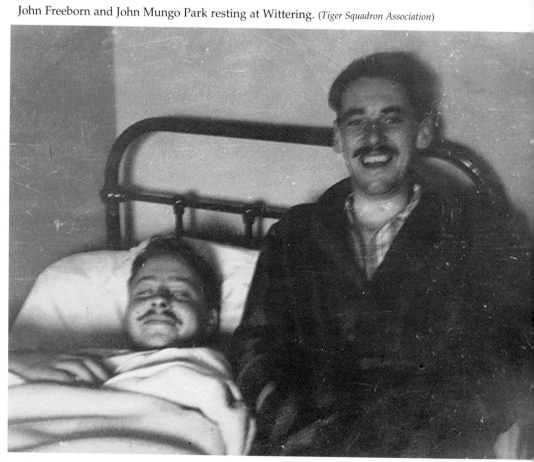

A 92 Squadron Spitfire being worked on at Biggin Hill. (*Michael Robinson*)

John Freeborn wearing his Distinguished Flying Cross. (*Tiger Squadron Association*)

hn Freeborn with his mother Jean in Leeds shortly after he received the DFC. (*Tiger Squadron sociation*)

Wood, Mungo Park and Freeborn standing in front of a de Havilland Puss Moth. (*Tiger Squadron Association*)

John Freeborn holding Mungo's dog, Ben. (*Tiger Squadron Association*)

John standing outside The Crown at Knockholt pub while he was stationed at Biggin Hill. (*Tiger Squadron Association*)

The smiling Tigers. John is third from the left. (*Tiger Squadron Association*)

Wing Commander John Freeborn at North Weald in 2003 visiting the grave of Pilot Officer Montague Leslie Hulton-Harrop. (*E.M. Aitken*)

Measures. Both pilots succeeding in downing the light observation aircraft but not before the rear gunner managed to put a bullet into the CO's radiator. White had no choice but to force land his Spitfire on the airfield at Calais Marck. On his way down White radioed Freeborn (who was the Squadron Adjutant) and asked him to tell his wife that he was okay and would soon be returning home. When John touched down from the patrol that is exactly what he did.

With the German army rapidly advancing, a rescue operation for Laurie White was quickly prepared. The Station Commander at Hornchurch was Group Captain Bouchier and despite Malan's protests he selected 54 Squadron for the operation. The rescue was a great success thanks to Flight Lieutenant James Leathart who flew a two-seater Magister to collect White, with Pilot Officers Alan Deere and Johnny Allen flying Spitfires as fighter escort. Both Deere and Allen performed excellently in their roles. Fighting off a gaggle of Messerschmitt 109s that engaged, they destroyed three of them before returning back to base with the Tiger's CO.

Prior to the rescue operation taking place Sailor Malan was unhappy to say the least with the Group Captain's decision to let 54 Squadron collect Laurie White because he felt it should be a job for 74 Squadron to take care of their own. Instead the Tigers were to fly as top cover, where they saw very little. On briefing the pilots Steve Stephen recalls Malan saying, 'If anyone suddenly decides his engine is running rough on this show, or turns back for any reason, he'll have me to deal with!'[2] Needless to say, nobody had any problems on this operation.

With White safely back at home the next step was retrieving his Spitfire before it fell into enemy hands. Two of 74's ground crewmen were flown over to Calais in a Blenheim to fix the Spitfire but unfortunately they were captured by German troops who by now had taken the area.

On a later patrol Paddy Byrne was also lost to the Squadron on the 23 May. Patrolling near Clarmarais Wood, his engine and leg was hit by ground fire which forced him to crash land with

[2] *Sky Tiger* – Norman Franks 1980

thick black smoke trailing from his aircraft. He was immediately taken prisoner by the Germans and ended up in Stalag Luft III for the remainder of the war. As John recalls, one individual wanted to actually 'see the war', so they went down and ended up right over a German battery. John says that he could hear twenty millimetre shells whizzing past his cockpit. However, he managed to climb up and away from the situation but others were not as fortunate.

Seemingly unstoppable, the German war machine was rapidly chewing its way through Europe. The Panzer tank divisions and German infantry were beating back the Allies at an alarming rate which resulted in the British Expeditionary Force having to retreat to the French coast. Totally surrounded by the German army the British troops began to flee to the beaches of Dunkirk. Now with their backs pressed desperately against the wall, the Channel was now the British army's only possible hope of escape. But curiously on the 24 May, Hitler ordered his tank divisions to halt their advance, leaving it up to Göring's *Luftwaffe* to finish off the encircled British troops. It was on this very day that 74 Squadron was back in action.

John doesn't ever recall seeing the soldiers down on the beaches, waiting to be rescued, because his patrol height was always at such a high altitude. When the evacuation operation at Dunkirk was in full effect thousands of men waited desperately by the shores as hundreds of sea vessels sailed towards them. Some troops were already wading in the water at their approach, while others ran for cover as German aircraft made relentless passes at them. Thick black smoke was seen rising further and further into the sky above where the Tigers had problems of their own.

During the patrols made throughout the day the Squadron lost Flying Officer Sammy Hoare who was forced to land at Calais due to a glycol leak. He was later captured by the Germans and became a prisoner of war. Sergeant Pilot Tony Mould went missing and Flight Lieutenant Paddy Treacy baled out of a burning Spitfire. Both men made their way back to English shores by boat. Flying Officer John Mungo Park was also slightly wounded in the arm during combat over the coast.

Down on the frantic beaches, Stuka dive bombers and German fighter planes were causing chaos amongst the retreating troops. The latter frequently indulged in unmerciful strafing runs, causing havoc amongst the stranded soldiers. Perhaps it was this brutality which caused Freeborn to return the sentiment. When a Ju 88 was shot down by the Tigers it crashed into a field and went right through a herd of unsuspecting cows. Freeborn flew low as the German crew staggered out of their broken aircraft, angrily shaking their fists at the Spitfires circling above them. Abruptly ending their irate gestures, Pilot Officer Freeborn swooped down with all guns blazing and put the crew out of their misery.

It is worth pausing for a brief moment to explain that sadly John's log books were lost during the war, so unsurprisingly the different accounts whether official, unofficial or John's own, occasionally conflict regarding certain dates and claims.

Although the actual day remains forgotten it was during the daily patrols along the French coast that John Freeborn found himself in a worrying predicament over enemy occupied territory. After shooting sheer hell into a Ju 88, John's Spitfire was hit in the bottom petrol tank by return fire which put him in an uncomfortable position. 'It obviously hit me in my bottom tank because I quickly ran out of fuel. I looked over the side at the sea below and thought bugger that, I'll try and put it down instead. So that's what I did'. John made a decent forced landing in France and hurriedly unstrapped himself before climbing out of the cockpit. Aware that the country was rapidly filling up with the German army, John had some quick thinking to do. The first thing he did was push his Spitfire into the undergrowth nearby. Then, to make sure that his aircraft would be concealed from the air as well as the ground he began to cover the Spitfire with branches until he was satisfied that it was well hidden. Then briefly scanning his surroundings, John set off on a mission to see if he could secure some petrol from the French locals with hopes that he would be able to refill his tanks and make his way back to England across the Channel. The task at hand was difficult to say the least. The stranded pilot spent three days eluding the Germans, desperately trying to obtain some petrol. He was tired, he was hungry, he was frightened and he didn't want to be a prisoner. Finally John caught sight of a German fuel supply tanker that had been left behind by the enemy. Seizing the opportunity John leapt into the supply tanker and thought 'How do I start this damn thing?' Soon enough he got it started and accelerated to the field where his Spitfire was left hidden, feeling thrilled with his discovery. 'I hadn't thought about how I was going to get the petrol from the tanker into the Spitfire', but it wasn't to matter. John's keen blue eyes had spotted a German column coming towards him. With nothing left to do but run, John left his Spitfire and managed to hide in a nearby cemetery. 'I hid behind monuments and gravestones under machine-gun fire, but they didn't know where I was, so I managed to slip away. I walked all the way back to Calais. My feet were sore in my flying boots so I cut the tops in half with my penknife, but they were not made for walking'.

Soon after reaching Calais John managed to hitch a ride back to England in a Blenheim, thoroughly relieved!

On 24 May, 74 Squadron flew their patrol line along the Hook of Holland and down to Calais in search of the enemy. 'I hated that journey', John says, taking a moment to remember it, 'I hated all journeys over the sea'. As the Tigers cruised high above the ships below them they encountered a formation of Dornier 17s and got stuck in. Malan latched onto one of the bombers which kept dipping in and out of cloud cover. He managed to fire a series of short deflection bursts which set its starboard engine on fire. By this time Malan's ammunition had been expended, so the rest of his section moved in and shot at the Do 17, sending it spiralling down to earth in flames.

Later in the afternoon the boys were back in the air flying just off the coast of Dunkirk where they saw anti-aircraft fire bursting into the air above them. Malan led the Squadron up to investigate and sure enough they sighted three formations of Heinkel 111s. Climbing through heavy flak, the Tigers attacked the middle formation of Heinkels. One of the He 111s was knocked out of the formation by anti-aircraft fire, Malan latched onto another and shot at both engines before being shaken by an anti-aircraft shell that bolted through his starboard wing. By this time Freeborn had become separated from his section. He looked up towards the sun to see Messerschmitt 109s and 110s diving towards them like eagles to their prey. Taking evasive action he escaped their sharp claws and soon after managed to get behind a 109.

The Messerschmitt 109 was an impressive aircraft that soon earned the respect of its opponents. Its dimensions were slightly smaller and its speed just that little bit faster than that of the Spitfire; however in combat both had its advantages over the other, as John would soon discover. The Spitfire's engine had a carburettor, so when it was put into a steep dive the flow of fuel would cease and the aircraft would lose engine power, but the 109's engine was fuel-injected which enabled it to carry on at full power. This meant that if a Spitfire was diving after a 109, its engine would stall and the 109 could easily escape. Nevertheless, the Spitfire had a superior turning circle than the 109, so it could usually turn inside the 109 and end up on its tail in a dogfight.

Lining the 109 up in his gun sight Freeborn waited for the right moment before thumbing the gun button. He fired a three second deflection shot and watched his bullets tear into the metal of the 109. He could see that it was in a spot of bother but had to duck out from the engagement due to another 109 preparing itself for an attack on him.

On landing back at Hornchurch John was greeted by his faithful fitter who helped him out of the cockpit looking as excited as ever to learn of his success. John's official combat report reads as follows:

> I was flying as No. 2. Red Section 'A' Flight No. 74 Squadron. Whilst on Patrol A.A. fire was noticed and we saw a formation of nine He 111s flying west at 12,000 feet followed by another formation of approximately 12 to 15 He 111s and Do 17s. We were flying at 500 feet when A.A. fire was first noticed and we climbed to 13,000 in line astern. As we came into range of the second wave, Red Leader ordered 'Echelon Port'. I then attacked an He 111 and got a two seconds burst in, starting at 300 yards, and finishing at 100 yards. Due to a large overtaking speed I had to break away. As I broke away

two Me 109s got onto my tail; I dived steeply with the two e/a following me, one was on my tail and the other on my port quarter. As I dived to ground level I throttled back slightly and the e/a on my tail overshot me and I was able to get a three seconds burst at a range of about 50 to 100 yards. [It] seemed to break away slowly to the right as though he was badly hit and I think that he crashed. The second Me 109 then got onto my tail but I got away from it using the boost cut-out.

On the 27 May, the Tigers would again meet up with the *Luftwaffe's* finest menace and be thrust into another day of heavy fighting. At 8,000 feet the Squadron spotted at least 15 Messerschmitt 109s flying through broken cloud with plenty of cover around them. In a matter of seconds the sky was full of aircraft tearing through the air in all directions. The melee of combat had exploded once again. Momentarily Freeborn picked out his target and swiftly managed to latch onto the tail of a 109. After some tricky twisting and turning, Freeborn lined the 109 up in his gun sight and fired a short burst which peppered the aircraft in front. Ever aware of the dangers around him, Freeborn pulled firmly back on the control column and shot up through cloud cover to gain height. As the Spitfire's nose emerged from the cumulous Freeborn looked out in panic to see three 109s diving down at him. Spinning round, he dived back into the cloud from which he had surfaced and steeply descended at an incredible rate of speed. Having lost his pursuers in the thick white cloud he emerged from the bottom to see a Spitfire being tailed by a 109. Freeborn steered his aircraft after the bandit and quickly appeared behind its tail. The 109 must have seen him because it immediately took evasive action. The German pilot rammed his stick forward putting the Messerschmitt into a steep dive knowing full well that the Spitfire couldn't emulate the manoeuvre due to its lack of fuel injection. Knowing that the Spitfire's engine would cut out if he dived after the 109 at such a sharp angle, Freeborn half rolled the Spitfire and followed it down through cloud. When he dropped out of the bottom of the cumulous Freeborn saw the 109 right in front of him. 'He kept flying straight and level but he was losing height, so I kept giving him a little burst to help him down'. Flying steadily behind the Messerschmitt Freeborn kept his thumb lightly on the gun button and watched as the 109 faltered. 'The engine stopped and the propeller was just windmilling'. Close enough to see the German pilot, John recalls, 'He looked bloody terrified. I thought, you German bastard, and I gave him another one. He hit a telegraph pole with the prop and went straight into a farmhouse'.[3] John watched as the 109 crashed right through the farmhouse and out the other side. A farmer ploughing his field outside angrily shook his fist at Freeborn as he climbed away. Then like a bolt of lightning the thought struck John that whoever was inside that house would surely be dead, and he felt sick. Over sixty years later, John still carries a deep remorse for that tragic incident, however unavoidable it may have been. The danger of this trip was not yet over for Freeborn. On his return to Hornchurch Freeborn encountered a different problem than enemy fighters.

> I was flying back to Hornchurch at about 10,000 feet across the French coast and I was shot at right, left and centre. I've never seen so many shells in all my life. There were five destroyers. Four of them were shooting at me and the fifth had been severely damaged by bombs. As a result the Royal Navy took it out on me, which of course was typical. You would escort them and go off for a bit and then when you were leaving they'd open fire on you! I don't blame them really, but they thought every aircraft was German.

John's official combat report for this encounter reads as follows:

> I was Red 2 on Offensive Patrol – Calais–Dunkerque at various heights from 200–15,000 feet owing to cloud formation. Sighted four Me 109s at 12–15,000 feet. Red 1 ordered

[3] *Fighter Boys*, Patrick Bishop, 2003

section to break into pairs. I attacked with Red 4. Attacked 2nd Me 109 from line astern, followed through cloud firing several bursts at 200 yards–150 yards range. Observed my fire to be effective, tracer entering fuselage. E/a broke away left with very heavy black smoke and flame coming out of engine. I then climbed and saw three more Me 109s; they attacked me, so I half rolled into cloud and lost them. Coming out of cloud I saw one Me 109 shooting on tail of Spitfire. I got one short deflection shot at 50 yards. E/a half rolled into cloud and I followed, his evasive tactics were very low flying (5 feet). [It] tried to fly me into obstacles, but I was about 20 feet above and on his starboard quarters. I followed and gave several short bursts. E/a hit a field at 300 m.p.h. and I saw him fly again for 1,000 yard[s], he then flew into a telegraph pole in the next field and into a farmhouse.

Later in the Mess the mood was sombre. 74 Squadron had lost Paddy Treacy for a second time. No one had seen him go down and it wasn't until much later that his whereabouts became known. On a patrol with his flight, Treacy soon gave battle to three Dornier 17s off Calais. Sergeant Pilot Bill Skinner took care of one and Treacy downed a second before chasing the third deep into enemy lines. The Irishman watched as the Do 17 dived with its port engine aflame but was imminently distracted by the smell of glycol in his own cockpit. Heading for the beaches of Dunkirk he was hit by flak which forced him to land with his wheels retracted near the Belgian coast. He was taken prisoner by the Germans, roughed up a bit and then put in a prisoners camp where he met Wing Commander Sir Basil Embry.

One morning when the prisoners were being transferred to another camp, the two airmen suddenly disappeared from the column by diving into a ditch. Becoming separated, both men made a run for it. After evading the Germans for over a week, Treacy was again captured by the Nazis and remained a prisoner for a mere two hours. Again the Irishman was on the move. He managed to hide in a Frenchwoman's house for several days where he was given food, money and a bicycle by the French

Resistance. John can't help but smile at the thought of dear old Treacy riding the tyres off that bicycle shouting, 'Which way to Marseille?'. Eventually the persistent Tiger managed to secure a rowing boat from a Frenchman and sure enough he was away, rowing his arms off towards England. John finds the image of an Irishman trying to find his way to England in a rowing boat naturally amusing, but what happened next was anything but funny. As Treacy heard the sound of engines nearby, his heart skipped a beat to discover that he was being followed by two Messerschmitt 110s. Treacy dived overboard as the 110s opened fire and sprayed the boat with bullets. He managed to hide underneath it for protection but soon enough his luck had run out and he was retrieved by a German motor-boat. The adventures of Paddy Treacy's marvellous escapes alone are enough to fill a book, but suffice it to say that yet again he escaped from captivity and made it back to England. Soon after his return he left 74 Squadron and was given command of 242 Squadron. Sadly, in April 1941, Paddy Treacy was killed in a mid-air collision with his wingman. 'Both were killed. It was very sad after all Treacy had gone through'.

In a matter of days the battle of Dunkirk concluded with a miraculous feat of 338,226 men being successfully evacuated from France on 4 June, 1939. The tremendous evacuation effort was carried out by a great number of sea vessels ranging from private boats and commercial ships to fishing boats and naval vessels that made numerous trips up and down the Thames to rescue the encompassed troops at Dunkirk. This marvellous event was a great morale boost for Britain as a whole, although the RAF took a lot of flak from the army, who claimed not to have seen them during their struggle on the beaches.

Although perhaps not seen by the troops thousands of feet below, 74 Squadron alone had proven their presence in the air by destroying 19 enemy aircraft with additional probabilities and several others damaged. Victories aside, their losses were also evidence of their contribution as fighter support.

Pilot Officer Freeborn, along with his companions, was completely exhausted having flown at least four sorties a day, patrolling over Boulogne, Calais, St Omer and Dunkirk where they were engaged in furious battles with the Hun. The pilots, like their aircraft, were worn out. The reality of war was ever present in their minds. The Squadron had now suffered injury, death and lost friends and familiar faces to German prison camps, but despite such adversity these young pilots were forced to suppress such thoughts and realisations for their own well being. An important job was at hand and that was all that mattered. Such ability to quash their fears, despite them being real, was bravery in its truest form.

After the strenuous events of the 27th, the Squadron was withdrawn from Hornchurch for a much needed rest. They would return from Leconfield on 6 June, with Sailor Malan having been awarded the DFC and John Freeborn being promoted as a Flight Commander. In reflection of the previous month, 74 Squadron had now proven themselves to be an aggressive fighter unit with strong pilots that never shirked from danger. Already their achievements were most commendable and their courage supreme.

Just a short while ago, eighteen year old John Freeborn set foot in Hornchurch wondering what the coming months would bring. Now he knew: the then fresh-faced pilot now looked slightly older and evidently more tired. His ocean blue eyes now looked deeper from experience and somehow less bright. The young tiger of 74 Squadron had grown up fast over Dunkirk, becoming a cub no more.

During this brief window of rest and recovery from their labours the Squadron was promised to be re-equipped with Spitfire MK IIs, but on their return to Rochford they were disappointed to learn that the arrival of new aircraft would be delayed. On a positive note, their current Spitfire MK Is had been fitted with armour plating behind the seats and bullet-proof windscreens had been installed at the front of their cockpits.

The time out from battle had given the Squadron an opportunity to reassess their tactics and to develop and incorporate new methods into their training. Sailor Malan and his Flight Commanders quickly began to recognise the disadvantages of the current vic three formations they were using. While this formation was fine for the leader, the two wingmen had to concentrate so much on staying tight, but at a safe distance from their leader, that they had barely any freedom to search the sky for enemy aircraft. A flaw such as this was unforgivable in aerial combat because failing to spot the enemy would result in catastrophe. Instead, it was decided to fly in finger four formations which proved much looser and more efficient in combat. The harmonisation of their guns was also realigned to their acquired requests. John remembers most having their ammunition set to converge at 250 yards ahead of the Spitfire. This setting became the general rule of thumb throughout fighter squadrons, although John preferred his to be set at 100 yards.

June proved to be fairly quiet in comparison with the previous month. France had now fallen and Britain knew full well that she was next on Hitler's agenda. A time for re-equipping and rearming was now in force on both sides of the Channel. Air activity filtered out after Dunkirk, although the *Luftwaffe* did continue to probe Britain's airspace by making reconnaissance runs and flying night patrols. For the duration of this lull before the storm, the men of 74 Squadron began to operate at night in search of enemy aircraft. These night patrols consisted of individual flights and were usually ineffective due to lack of visibility, the pilots relied solely on instruments and searchlights alone. However on a night sortie on the 18/19 June, Sailor Malan shot down two Heinkel 111s earning a bar to his DFC.

It was also in the month of June that Malan visited the Royal Aircraft Establishment (RAE) at Farnborough where he was asked with several other pilots to fly a Messerschmitt 109E-3 that had been previously captured by the French. The German fighter belonged to JG54 and was wrongly landed in an orchard at Woerth, Bas-Rhin, by its pilot, who thought he was over friendly ground. The 109 was fully intact and had been handed over to the British.

Five days prior to Malan's arrival at Farnborough, Bob Stanford Tuck flew the 109 in a mock dogfight with a Spitfire to evaluate its performance and now Malan would do the same. The opportunity to test and study their adversary was naturally a welcomed advantage.

With the Battle of France well and truly over Britain stood alone against Nazi Germany, outnumbered and unprepared. Ultimately, all that was standing between invasion and occupation were fighter pilots like John Freeborn.

'The Battle of France is over', Winston Churchill declared ... 'I expect The Battle of Britain is about to begin'.

Illustration by David Pritchard

CHAPTER FIVE

The Battle of Britain

In the early summer of 1940, *Reichmarschall* Hermann Göring with his senior *Luftwaffe* officers and staff stood on the coast near Calais and looked out across the Channel towards Britain. There on the horizon was the thin line of the English coast, home to 35 RAF squadrons, equipped with approximately 650 fighter aircraft. The ill-equipped, lonely island of Britain was left to stand against an experienced German bomber and fighter force of about 3,500 aircraft.

Hitler, having failed to frighten Britain into submission ordered Göring's *Luftwaffe* to pave the way for a preconceived invasion of Britain codenamed Operation Sealion. Hitler knew that unless the RAF was neutralised, a sea and land assault on Britain would be impossible. The overconfidence and arrogance of the German leaders boasted that they would have air superiority over Fighter Command in a matter of days, but thanks to the brave men and woman of Britain, it was simply not to be.

The Battle of Britain lasted from the 10 July 1940 until the 31 October 1940. It was during this long hot summer and autumn that the fate of Britain was to be decided.

On the 10 July 1940, John was shaken awake by his batman at an ungodly hour in the morning. The young pilot forced himself out of bed and made his way down to dispersal where he would wait with the other pilots of 74 Squadron. The dark Wednesday morning turned out to be a miserable affair. The south of England was covered in thick thunderous cloud accompanied by heavy rain.

As John sat in dispersal watching his fellow chums reading or dozing in their chairs he wondered when the shrill sound of the telephone would ring. As Squadron Adjutant John had already made up the board for the morning, informing the pilots who would be flying and in what section etc. Malan, as usual, had scanned the board and nodded his approval, so for now all there was to do was wait. Being ordered to 'scramble' became a daily occurrence for the fighter pilots. It was never a pleasant experience for any of them, and it was never something one got used to. Some would run to their aircraft feeling full of anxiety and apprehension, while others would throw up before climbing into their machines. John eventually found he was able to cope with the strenuous routine by knowing that as soon as he got airborne and fuelled with adrenaline, he would be able to get on with the job at hand.

The *Luftwaffe*'s opening attacks on Britain were concentrated on shipping convoys positioned in the English Channel and on the southern coastal ports of Britain. On the morning of the 10 July, a convoy rounding the North Foreland became of particular interest to a Dornier 17 reconnaissance aircraft, escorted by an entire group of Bf 109s. To counteract the invasion six Spitfires of 74 Squadron were scrambled from nearby Manston. At 20,000 feet the Tigers caught up with the enemy but due to the great number of fighter escort keeping everybody busy, the Dornier slipped away across the Channel. John remembers this skirmish over the Thames Estuary well: 'I was so close to the leader of this formation of 109s that I could see everything that hit him when I opened fire. He turned straight over on his back and dropped into the sea'.

Freeborn turned his head to look behind and caught sight of a 109 on his tail being pursued by a Spitfire. To evade the 109's cannon shells, Freeborn put his aircraft into a stall turn with hopes of shaking the enemy off and getting onto his rear quarter so he could shoot him down. However, before he had a chance to attack the 109 he had other worries. 'I saw a Spitfire with sparkling wings. He was shooting at the 109 but he missed the bloody thing and hit me! He shot my top petrol tank which caused petrol to go everywhere. I switched off anything that was electrical and could spark and glided into Manston'. Having safely landed the aircraft, John unstrapped himself and pushed the cockpit hood back.

I was sitting by my aircraft waiting for someone to come and pick me up and I saw Tony Mould come in to land. I thought 'Bloody hell where's he been?' He was like a flying sieve when he went passed me; he'd been hit by everything! As he came in he started falling to pieces, the poor Spitfire couldn't take anymore and it just collapsed. He got out and I said, 'You dosey bugger! Didn't you know you'd been hit?' because he side slipped his Spitfire in and made a right botched landing. 'Did you know you hit me?' John asked as Tony walked towards him. 'I didn't know. You shouldn't have been there! It was a 109 I was after'. 'Did you get the 109?' 'Of course I damn well did', Tony replied. 'You got two on that bloody trip then because you got me as well', John remarked. Poor old Tony. He was a Sergeant Pilot and he was a good one. He was a great credit to 74 Squadron and he was a great pal of mine. We spent a lot of time together.

The combat report John wrote after the dogfight reads differently than as told above, perhaps to save face for Mould.

I was flying as Red Leader, leading 'A' Flight No. 74 Squadron. I was ordered to patrol base and then sent to investigate bombing of a convoy 2 miles east of Deal. Four bombs were dropped near to the convoy but no direct hits. I was then ordered to patrol convoy. I was flying at 12,000 ft. and I saw two aircraft. I then climbed for height and saw a Do 17 or Do 215 escorted by 30 Me 109s. I had advantage of height and ordered 'line astern' and attacked the Me 109s as they climbed to attack. I engaged one enemy aircraft and opened fire at approximately 50 yards. My bullets entered the enemy aircraft and seemed to knock it sideways. This aircraft then just 'dropped out of the sky' and was seen to go down out of control by Observers at Manston. I then turned to attack another Me 109 and I myself was then attacked by another Me 109. This latter enemy aircraft was taken off my tail by Red 2. Several other enemy aircraft got on to my tail. These were very easy to shake off, but due to superior numbers I could not shake them all off. I was finally shot down by enemy aircraft and I made a successful forced landing at Manston aerodrome.

Due to the heavy attacks being mounted by the *Luftwaffe*, the fighter boys were needed at almost every waking hour to compensate for the lack of qualified pilots and equipment that Britain so desperately needed. The coming weeks ahead would be strenuously demanding for Fighter Command and the pilots of 74 Squadron were needed more than ever. In the Battle of Britain John Freeborn flew more operational hours than any other pilot during this time of conflict.

An average day started about half an hour to an hour before first light and so in the summer time it was a long day. My batman would wake me up and I'd go and eat some breakfast, then go straight down to the dispersal point where we'd literally get things moving. When the phone would ring and we heard 'Scramble' we'd jump out of our bloody uniforms and run to our aircraft. I was frightened, but once I got airborne I'd soon settle down. Then you would see the specs in the sky and you knew what they were.

The reconnaissance Dornier 17 that had escaped across the Channel was undoubtedly shot up by somebody because it limped back to France carrying dead and wounded crew members. Nonetheless the *Luftwaffe* now knew the convoy's position and later in the afternoon they sent another raid to attack it. Just after

1330 hours Fighter Command began to plot the first signs of enemy build-up over Pas de Calais. The enemy was coming and British fighter pilots were rushing towards their aircraft. By the time eight Spitfires from 74 Squadron had been scrambled, 32, 56 and 111 Squadrons were already airborne over the convoy. A mass raid of approximately 26 Dornier 17s, accompanied by Messerschmitt 110s and 109s was fast approaching and soon enough an angry dogfight ensued. Tigers Mungo Park, Peter St. John, Ben Draper, Tinky Measures and Peter Stevenson all laid claim on the enemy. New Zealander Don Cobden damaged a Dornier but was reported to have force landed at Manston due to battle damage.

> *Don Cobden was not the best of pilots because he wouldn't take to being told what to do and he had to bloody say so. Ernie Mayne and I used to tell him something and he'd say, 'You two have got some queer ideas'. Don was an All Black Rugby player before the war with 28 caps for his country. He was a charming bloke and he'd do anything to upset me. He would get into my aircraft and I'd soon shout, 'You're not using my bloody aeroplane!' 'Oh yes I am', he'd say, 'I've got to fly something and yours will do'. But being 6 foot odd he would put the pedals right forward so that it was more comfortable for him and when I'd get into it, I couldn't even reach the pedals, I could barely see them they were so bloody far forward! Don would have the greatest pleasure when he came back from a trip in saying, 'That aeroplane of yours does fly well!'*
>
> *I always flew 'ZPC' and when I was in 118 Squadron I flew 'JHC', I always flew 'C' and I have no idea why because it was originally Byrne's bloody aeroplane. You see every aeroplane, like motor cars, are different. Little bits and pieces are different and its these little differences on a Spitfire that you got used to, therefore you were more comfortable flying your own aeroplane.*

On 12 July, the Germans continued to harass the Channel convoys that were steaming along in the Thames Estuary. Several squadrons tangled with the *Luftwaffe* throughout the day, engaging in fierce dogfights high above the ships. It wasn't until the late afternoon that Red Section of 74 Squadron was called into action. Taking off from Manston, Sailor Malan led Mould and Stevenson to the north-east of Margate where they shot down a Heinkel 111 after it had dropped its bombs onto one of the sea vessels below. To the seamen's greatest delight they watched the He 111 plunge into the sea.

The 24 July brought a vast amount of cloud over the south coast of England along with enemy aircraft intent on disturbing the Channel ports. Once again the Tigers were found leaping into the thick of it. Six Merlin Spitfire engines roared across the aerodrome at Manston with Freeborn leading 'A' Flight. The Flight of Spitfires climbed to their vectored height and began to patrol the Channel for enemy raiders. As they made their approach to Dover, they sighted three Dornier Do 215s flying at sea level about 2,000 yards away. Both Red and Yellow sections sped towards the Do 215s at full throttle but were soon opened up on by their rear gunners. The Dorniers broke off for the French coast, firing their MG15 machine guns at their attackers. Freeborn's Red Section, consisting of Don Cobden and Douglas Hastings, managed to get within a range of approximately 300 yards before raking one of the Dornier's with their bullets. Freeborn saw his ammunition 'enter his wings and fuselage'. By this time they were much too close to the French coast, so wisely, the Spitfires broke away leaving the Do 215s to fly back home relatively intact.

Earlier in the day, 74's neighbouring Squadron, 54, lost two Spitfires in combat. Pilot Officer Johnny Allen, DFC, was shot down and killed by a Messerschmitt 109 near North Foreland and Sergeant Pilot G.R. Collet force landed with minor injuries.

Flight Lieutenant Measures left 74 Squadron on the same day. He was posted to No. 7 Operational Training Unit as an instructor.

On 28 July, the *Luftwaffe* droned through the fine Sunday weather like a black cloud destined to rain fire upon the South of England. To counteract the threat the Sector Controllers ordered twelve Spitfires of 74 Squadron off from Manston with instructions to engage the fighter escort, while a squadron of Hurricanes concentrated their attacks on the bombers. As Malan led the Squadron in tight formation to their position they were bounced by 36 Messerschmitt 109s of *Jagdgeschwader* JG 51, led by Major Werner Mölders. A savage dogfight followed with Malan giving his instructions to Freeborn who was leading Yellow Section. 'Malan ordered my section to try and draw them off, so I broke away'. Within seconds Pilot Officer James Young flying at Freeborn's side was shot out of the sky and killed and then moments later Sergeant Pilot Tony Mould was wounded and was forced to bale out of his aircraft. Everything was happening so fast, Freeborn was now alone and he had to think quickly if he was going to get out of this alive. Pulling his Spitfire up towards a 109, he decided to shadow it by flying closely underneath the Messerschmitt in the hope of avoiding being attacked by the hordes of enemy fighters out for his blood. Not wanting to hit their own aircraft the Germans held their fire until the 109 Freeborn was using as insurance suddenly pulled away. Freeborn lifted the Spitfire's nose and fired a three second burst. The 109 exploded into a terrific ball of flame at about 18,000 feet which sent his victim's comrades into a flurry of rage as they thundered towards him with their cannons blazing. Rolling his aircraft, Freeborn dived away towards Brighton Pier trying desperately to escape the wrath of the diving 109s as their cannon shells battered his aircraft. Bullet after bullet chewed through his Spitfire, smashing the canopy and shattering his gun sight. Glass exploded everywhere but fortunately his goggles protected his wide blue eyes and his gloves protected his sweaty hands from the fragments. The Spitfire's engine had blown up from the 109s unrelenting attacks but by now he was clocking a speed of about 400mph and was able to glide his aircraft back into Manston. His rudder had been badly damaged, causing it to lock to the left so, when Freeborn landed his wing-tip dug into the grass and the Spitfire tipped up onto its nose but then fell back down onto its wheels. The ground crew ran to his aircraft and pulled John out of the cockpit and gasped at the sight of him being covered in blood from the hundreds of glass fragments embedded in his skin. The wounded pilot, who had narrowly escaped death, was whisked away to sick bay where the glass was removed. While John was being treated for his injuries the ground crew inspected his Spitfire. They found nineteen bullet dents in the armour plating that had been recently installed behind his head. John is not exactly sure why the 109s broke off their attack on this occasion, but it could have been that they thought he was done for, or that they themselves were vulnerable to an attack. Reflecting upon this experience, John recalls: 'That day I couldn't find my flying helmet. I usually kept it on the stick you see, but it wasn't there so I grabbed Mungo Park's instead. After being clobbered by those German bastards, the helmet was torn to bits and soaked in blood.' On John's return from the sick bay Mungo said, 'Freeborn, next time, wear your own bloody helmet!' Of course, he was delighted to see his old pal safe.

An hour later, after John had crash-landed and been treated for his injuries, he was back in the air leading another patrol, this time with his own helmet on. The previous encounter with JG 51 was not without incident for Malan's Red Section either. Malan managed to turn onto the tail of a 109 and gave it a succession of short bursts from about 250 to 100 yards. The 109 decreased its speed and made a gentle right-hand turn. Concluding that its controls had probably been damaged, Malan broke off noticing another 109 preparing to get onto his tail. Malan turned so sharply into the attack that he was able to spray the 109's fuselage and tail before running out of ammunition. The 109, later discovered to have been flown by the elite German fighter pilot, Werner Mölders, managed to crash-land his aircraft at Wissant. The German pilot was wounded from the Tiger's attack. In total the boys of 74 had shot down three 109s and damaged two others during this action but had sadly lost Pilot Officer Young. Wounded, Tony Mould managed successfully to bale out of his Spitfire and was taken to the Dover Military Hospital to recover.

On 31 July, the *Luftwaffe* continued to penetrate British airspace through the hazy weather. In the early evening the Dover balloon barrage was continually strafed by enemy fighters, thought to have been making an entrance to the harbour for a later attack. Several Spitfire and Hurricane squadrons were ordered to Dover to fend off the fighters but only 74 Squadron caught up with them. Already airborne from Manston, Freeborn led Yellow Section into a head-on attack against a large number of Bf 109s that were approaching from the coast at about 18,000 feet. As the Tigers ploughed towards them in their Spitfires, the enemy aircraft broke away and scattered into cloud. Catching sight of some 109s heading back across the sea, Freeborn gave chase and fired a long burst from 500 yards closing to 200 yards. His bullets scored direct hits and sparkled across the metal frame of the 109 causing it to dive steeply towards the sea trailing smoke. Freeborn watched as the 109 pressed on towards the French coast but he made the decision to break away. Just seconds before he had seen Pilot Officer Harold Gunn being attacked by two 109s and so he veered round to help him, but it was too late. Gunn's Spitfire had been shot down into the sea. Gunn was not the only casualty from Blue Section on this encounter. Sergeant Pilot F.W. Eley was shot down and killed over Folkestone harbour and Blue Leader Piers Kelly's aircraft was heavily damaged by 109s. The latter managed to land at Manston where he was greeted by renowned Supermarine Test Pilot Jeffrey Quill, who could just not believe how much punishment Kelly's Spitfire was able to take.

The fighting around 'Hell's Corner' as it became known was beginning to take its toll on the fighter boys. However there was at least some cause to celebrate on the last day of July, for John Freeborn was awarded the Distinguished Flying Cross and Sailor Malan received a bar to his DFC.

In the first week of August, 74 Squadron received two additional members to their ranks. Flight Lieutenant Stanislaw Brzezina and Flying Officer Henryk Szczesny, two battle-hardened Polish pilots that were instantly nicknamed 'Breezy' and 'Sneezy' by the boys. John recalls Brzezina and Szczesny as possessing a strong hatred towards the Germans, a passion which manifested itself in the air. They were both fierce fighter pilots that were more than willing to lend a hand to the British after fleeing from their own country when the Germans invaded Poland. In due course, John's family came into contact with Szczensy's family and began corresponding by discreet letters.

Sadly the return letters stopped arriving and it was later learnt that Szczesny's family had been murdered in a Nazi gas chamber. The horrifying news caused considerable depression for poor Henryk.

As the battle wore on and new faces began appearing around the station, John, now well and truly battle-experienced, began to discern which pilots would survive and which pilots were unlikely to. It wasn't a pleasant attribute to harbour but it was there all the same. John was learning that experience was one of the most critical factors in survival and some young men just weren't awarded that luxury. The furnace of war was getting hotter by the day and more pilots were being lost. The need for replacement pilots rapidly increased but time was against them. 'Some of them couldn't cope with the Spitfire. The Spitfire coped with them, but they couldn't cope with it'.

On 8 August, Laurie White was posted to Fighter Command Headquarters and Sailor Malan was given command of the Squadron.

By the 11 August, the Germans ushered in the second phase of the Battle of Britain by changing their tactics from Channel attacks to coastal airfields. In the previous month the *Luftwaffe* had done their best to test the RAF's air defences to which Fighter Command had responded exceptionally well, but now the opening stages of the battle had drawn to a close. The real test was about to begin.

At dawn, Sailor Malan led twelve Spitfires of 74 Squadron up into the fine bright Sunday weather. Flying in astute formation the fighter boys climbed for height and levelled out for Dover, where they were vectored to intercept enemy aircraft assaulting the balloon barrages. By the time the Tigers arrived on the scene, seventeen Messerschmitt 110s had made a pass at the harbour and fled back across the Channel leaving the 109s to tackle with the fighters. The strafing and bombing runs over Dover were of little consequence to the *Luftwaffe* at this stage. Their main intention was to draw the RAF's fighters into the air where they could be destroyed.

At 20,000 feet, Malan took the Squadron into eighteen Bf 109s near Dover and gave them everything they deserved. The Tigers claimed eight 109s destroyed and a further four damaged. Pilot Officer Peter Stevenson bounced a 109 at about 15,000 feet giving it a two second deflection burst which sent the Messerschmitt into a vertical dive and straight into the drink. Squadron Leader Malan tailed a 109 that half-rolled into an evasive dive and sent it down in flames after a series of deflection shots. Flying Officer Mungo Park destroyed a 109 and damaged another as did Flying Officer Hastings. Pilot Officer H.M. Stephen destroyed two and damaged two others, Pilot Officer Smith and Flying Officer Nelson also claimed one each. Already it had been quite a morning!

74's only loss during this scrap was a Spitfire after Peter Stevenson was beat up by a 109 and forced to bale out into the cold sea below. For ninety, long cold minutes Stevenson floated in the sea, wearing his Mae West, waiting to be rescued, until he caught sight of an Air-Sea Rescue launch vessel in his proximity. Failing to attract its attention he fired his revolver into the air but to no avail. Feeling thoroughly agitated by the crew's lack of vigilance, Stevenson unloaded an entire magazine at the vessel, which soon caught the crew's full attention. The downed pilot was soon dragged from the tumultuous sea, living to fight another day. John was especially pleased that he made it back to base. 'You couldn't wish to know a nicer bloke than Stevenson. All he wanted to do was go out and find some birds'.

On the second sortie of the day, John Freeborn would also join the Tigers' tally when the Squadron dived into the midst of several groups of 109s halfway across the Channel. Freeborn followed a 109 down in a dive and opened fire. His bullets began tearing fragments off the 109 while others pelted into its coolant tank. The Messerschmitt went into a vertical dive, bleeding white smoke and Freeborn shot back up into the clouds for cover. John's combat report further illustrates the scene:

I was flying as Yellow Leader with No. 74 Squadron at 25,000 feet. We were flying towards Dover, when we sighted two Me 109s. Dysoe Leader attacked the first 109 and I attacked the 2nd. The E/A half rolled and dived towards Cape Griz Nez. I dived after it and fired several short bursts at 300 yards range, closing to 150 yards range. The E/A then began to break up. Pieces seemed to come off the fuselage and wings as my bullets entered the E/A. The E/A then went into a vertical dive with glycol coming from his radiator. I then returned to my base.

Before dinner John was back in the air leading the Tigers on their third sortie of the day. Their instructions were to cover a naval convoy off Dover, but communication became frustrated as some 'inept controller' positioned them over a thick cloud base at 32,000 feet. John recalls his conversation with the controller as something to this effect: 'Many bandits, many bandits ahead. Can you see them?' 'No, I haven't seen them. Where are these "many" bandits?' John replied. 'You should see them now, right ahead of you', the controller assured him. 'How many bandits?' John asked searching the sky and seeing nothing of the sort. 'Many bandits, you will see them', the controller reported. But of course they were in the wrong position and Freeborn began to lose patience. 'You are probably passing them', the controller continued. 'Oh you're a prick', John retorted. 'When I land, I'll come down there and ram my boot right up your arse!' 'Don't you swear on the radio!' the controller replied, 'There are young ladies present'. 'Adjust your bloody map because you don't know where they are, but I do', John remarked. 'Where are they?' the controller asked. 'I'm not bloody telling you', John said as he pushed forward on the stick. 'I was above 8/10ths of cloud and somewhere underneath the cloud was a convoy with 110s knocking the stuffing out of them and here I was at 32,000 feet!' The Tigers dived down through the thick cloud at an incredible rate of knots and emerged above the convoy 'Booty', where reports had been made of forty Messerschmitt 110s approaching. 'We went down into the cloud at such a rate we must have been doing 400mph. When we got through the cloud there were aircraft already in the sea'.

As Freeborn dived he saw an explosion out of the corner of his eye but he didn't have time to assess the situation because of the great number of Bf 110s swarming the sky. Surrounded by the enemy he thumbed the gun button allowing for a succession of short bursts which sprayed three 110s. Banking his aircraft with great determination, he quickly caught hold of a group of 110s forming a defensive circle. It was too late for one of them. At close range Freeborn fired a two to three second burst and knocked it out of the arena. There was no time to process his achievement for he suddenly found himself being attacked from astern by a 110. Taking decisive action Freeborn managed to come up from under the 110, firing a long burst. The enemy aircraft's tailplane completely broke up in the air and the 110 was last seen spiralling towards the sea. Running low on ammunition and fuel Freeborn ducked out and returned to Manston.

The official combat report John filed sheds further light on the action:

> I was leading 74 Squadron when it took off from Manston at 1145 hours to patrol a convoy off Clacton. While on patrol I sighted a formation of forty Me 110s in vics of three and four approaching the convoy below the clouds (8/10 heavy cumulus at 4,000 feet). I led the squadron in a diving attack into the defensive circle which the E/A formed. In the dive and climb which followed I fired at 3 E/A, and in each case saw my de Wilde ammunition registering hits. The combat then developed into a dog-fight in the course of which I was able to get on the tails of two E/A, in each case firing two 3 second bursts from 200 yards closing to 100 yards. In one case the E/A dived straight into the sea and in the other case the E/A pancaked on the sea and then sunk.

The Tigers had fared well. Mungo Park, Stephen, Skinner, Kirk, Nelson and Ernie Mayne also laid claim on the enemy but their success did not come without a price. Pilot Officer Don Cobden and Pilot Officer Dennis Smith had lost their lives. To this day John wonders if the explosion he saw when he first dropped out of cloud was the New Zealander colliding with a 110. His good friend Don Cobden was gone and, 'it was very, very upsetting. It was his 26th birthday ... and what an awful present'.

The lovable veteran Ernie Mayne also had a near miss with death when he blacked out during the battle and plunged 20,000 feet before coming to. As a result he burst both eardrums and sensibly was grounded.

The fierce day of fighting was not yet over for the exhausted pilots. An hour later they were patrolling Hawkinge aerodrome and Margate when they were vectored onto a formation of Ju 87 Stuka dive bombers escorted by twenty Bf 109s flying at 10,000 feet as top cover. Malan, leading Red Section, ordered Blue Section, led by Mungo Park, to engage the Stukas but due to radio interference the message was misunderstood and all eight Spitfires attacked the fighters. The Stukas escaped into cloud while the fighters mixed it up. Freeborn got stuck in and damaged a 109 before attacking another. His second attack blew fragments off the 109 before its propeller stopped turning and it dropped out of the air. Freeborn cast his eyes around the empty sky. Moments ago it was full of speeding aircraft and now he was alone. Such was the mystery of aerial combat.

The 11 August, was finally over for the Tigers. They had flown four challenging sorties and destroyed an incredible twenty-three enemy aircraft and damaged a further fourteen with an additional probable. No. 74's achievements did not go unnoticed. The Chief of the Air Staff, Sir Cyril Newall, sent the Squadron a telegram which read:

> A magnificent day's fighting 74 ... This is the way to keep the measure of the Boche. Mannock started it and you keep it up.

In the evening Winston Churchill arrived at Hornchurch to personally congratulate the Squadron and their irreplaceable ground crew, who had also worked extremely hard throughout the day keeping their aircraft refuelled and serviceable.

The following day the pilots of 74 Squadron were given a much needed break from operations and were able to rest from their labours at Hornchurch. The ground crews however worked around the clock getting their Spitfires back to full health by patching up bullet holes and repairing any damage they had sustained. It was on this same day that Manston aerodrome was bombed by the *Luftwaffe*, where 74 Squadron would have been had they not been stood down.

The 13 August, was *Adler Tag* (Eagle Day) for the Germans, the day in which the *Luftwaffe* would supposedly crush the British air defences to make way for their planned land invasion. In the early morning hours approximately seventy-four Dornier Do 17s took off with the intention of bombing the Isle of Sheppey in the Thames Estuary. The plan was to meet up with sixty Bf 110s that would act as fighter cover but they were ordered directly from Göring to postpone 'Eagle Day' until the afternoon due to the deteriorating weather conditions. The fighters heard the message loud and clear and returned to base but the Bomber Commander heard no such order and failed to abort. The Do 17s continued across the Channel droning towards the Kent coast without fighter support, but due to the bad weather not all was lost. The Observer Corps made inaccurate reports due to the poor visibility, which meant that of the five Squadrons scrambled to meet the raid, only one intercepted. That Squadron was 74. Having left Hornchurch to patrol Manston, the Tigers were soon vectored onto forty or so bombers approaching at 3,000 feet, just below cloud base. Going full throttle, the Tigers roared into action causing the Dorniers to scatter like frightened cattle. The boys, including Freeborn, managed to destroy six enemy aircraft, with another six claimed as probables and one damaged.

John's Combat Report for 13/08/40 reads:

> When the Squadron was engaging enemy bombers in the Estuary, I encountered two Do 17s. They were in very close formation but I was able to spray both of them with bullets and saw my de Wilde ammunition entering the E/A. I then broke away and saw a vic of three with an additional one just below the cloud base, 2, 500 ft. The single aircraft entered the cloud so I chased the other three towards the coast. I got on the tail of one and opening at 200 yards closed to 100 yards. I attacked from astern, using all my ammunition in about ten second burst. The enemy aircraft took no evasive action and the Do then dived straight into the sea. This must have been just off Burchington.

After signing his name, John added to his report in pen: 'This crash is confirmed by a searchlight post'.

Piers Kelly was leading B Flight at the time of this interception and he also attacked a vic of Dorniers. He managed to knock one out of the formation trailing smoke and began firing at a second, but was rudely interrupted from the return fire of the third Do 17 which put a bullet into his glycol tank. He pulled up and away from the bombers with fumes filling his cockpit and decided he ought to bale out but Malan had seen Kelly's quandary and instructed him over the R/T to follow him back to Manston. With Malan's guidance Kelly landed at the bomb cratered aerodrome without further incident.

Kelly was not the only pilot to find himself on the end of Dornier gun fire. Flight Lieutenant Brzezina or 'Breezy' had also come under fire. Giving one of the Do 17s in the rear formation a long burst he watched the bomber descend towards the sea with a smoking engine before engaging another at about 50 yards. An explosion suddenly sounded in his cockpit and his Spitfire began to fall towards the earth. The panic stricken Pole managed to bale out of his aircraft at approximately 2,000 feet where he made a safe parachute landing. Brzezina's fellow countrymen, Henryk, also known as 'Henry the Pole' also found himself in a spot of trouble when he couldn't lower his undercarriage. He was forced to land on his belly at West Malling, unhurt. Throughout the day the *Luftwaffe* came over by the hundreds in hopes of achieving *Adler Tag*, but the RAF bravely withstood their attacks and destroyed forty-five of their aircraft. In comparison, Fighter Command had lost only thirteen.

The powers that be decided that 74 Squadron needed a rest from their duties and so the Tigers were withdrawn from the front line and sent to Wittering to recuperate. It had been an intense month for John Freeborn and although fatigued, he wasn't too pleased about missing out on the action down south. Malan also seemed very unhappy about being withdrawn from the battle, but it was apparent that his pilots needed a break.

A week later, the boys moved from Wittering to Kirton-in-Lindsey in Lincolnshire where training commenced and new pilots arrived to join the Tigers' ranks. Amongst those to arrive were Pilot Officer Alan Ricalton, Pilot Officers Wally Churches and Bob Spurdle, who were sent from No.7 OTU and Flying Officers Walter Franklin and Roger Boulding, who had been posted from 142 Squadron.

During this brief respite for 74 Squadron, John Freeborn was promoted from Pilot Officer to Flight Lieutenant and on the 29 August, he was given command of 'A' Flight.

Further south, the RAF was being stretched to the limit as the fighting grew fiercer with larger and more frequent raids crossing the Channel. The *Luftwaffe* was now relentlessly attacking inland airfields around London with potent force and the fighter boys were on constant readiness. Whilst 74 Squadron were further north, their home station Hornchurch was bombed by large formations of He 111s and Ju 88s. The Squadron's advanced base, Manston, was also heavily hit by German bombs, which rendered it useless until repairs could be made. Thick black smoke and dust covered the aerodrome and the unfortunate casualties below.

In the first week of September, John called the new pilot, Bob Spurdle into his office and gave him some instructions. 'You're to take a replacement Spit to Hornchurch; they're running out of machines. The place is often bombed and strafed, so fly low and don't fool around. I'm getting rid of "L"; it's the last of the hand-pump undercarriage kites.'[4]

When Spurdle arrived at Hornchurch he witnessed first-hand the great damage inflicted by the bombers. There were shattered brick walls, broken, abandoned hangers and bomb craters all over the aerodrome. In fact, moments after Spurdle touched down a bomber raid flew over and he was forced to take cover in a nearby shelter, where he heard the awful thumping explosions of bombs all around Hornchurch.

A couple of days after John assumed command of 'A' Flight, two pilots of 'B' Flight were involved in a training accident, when two Spitfires collided in mid-air. Pilot Officer Wally Churches' aircraft cut the tail off Bill Skinner's Spitfire after pulling up from a practice head-on attack. The plan was to proceed in a head-on

---

[4] *The Blue Arena*, Bob Spurdle, 1995

attack, pull up over the top of the aircraft and then turn starboard to come round for an attack in line astern, but as Skinner pulled up, Churches' propeller chewed his tail off and sent him into an alarming spin from which he managed to bale out. With blood running down his face, Skinner landed in a nearby field with the remains of his Spitfire and was approached by two farmers holding shotguns. After convincing the farmers he wasn't a German, Skinner was put to bed in a farmhouse until an ambulance arrived. With a bent propeller, Wally Churches managed to put his Spitfire down into a field. Both pilots were extremely fortunate to survive the collision.

It was during this time at Kirton-in-Lindsey that Sailor Malan wrote his famous ten rules for air fighting, although John is quick to add that it developed after a series of discussions had by the Squadron rather than just coming from one person. Nevertheless, the principles involved, already being used by the Tigers, became a guideline for less experienced pilots in Fighter Command. The rules that were written are as follows:

Ten of my Rules for Air fighting

1. Wait until you see the whites of his eyes. Fire short bursts of one to two seconds, and only when your sights are definitely 'on'.

2. Whilst shooting, think of nothing else. Brace the whole of the body, have both hands on the stick, concentrate on your ring sight.

3. Always keep a sharp look out. 'Keep your finger out!'

4. Height gives *you* the initiative.

5. Always turn and face the attack.

6. Make your decisions promptly. It is better to act quickly, even though your tactics are not the best.

7. Never fly straight and level for more than 30 seconds in the combat area.

8. When diving to attack, always leave a portion of your formation above to act as top guard.

9. Initiative, aggression, air discipline, and team-work
   are words that *mean* something in air fighting.
10. Go in quickly. Punch hard. Get out!

On 3 September, John Freeborn and Sailor Malan travelled
to Buckingham Palace to receive their DFCs. Naturally, it was
not just a memorable day for John but also for his parents,
Harold and Jean, who watched with pride as their son received
the Distinguished Flying Cross from King George VI. John's
official citation read:

> *This officer has taken part in nearly all offensive patrols
> carried out by his Squadron since the commencement of
> the war including operations over the Low Countries and
> Dunkirk and more recently engagements over the Channel
> and South East of England. During this intensive period of
> air warfare he had destroyed four enemy aircraft. His high
> courage and exceptional abilities as a leader have materially
> contributed to the notable successes and high standard of
> efficiency maintained by his Squadron.*

Of course by this time John had destroyed more than four
enemy aircraft, but when his DFC was first awarded several
months ago, this was the case.

The time for resting, training and re-equipping had quickly
come to an end for 74 Squadron. The battle in the south of
England was raging and the Tigers were needed back in the fray.
Some pilots in particular were keen to get back to the front line,
not because they were overcome with madness but because they
wanted to keep busy and break out of the monotony of training.
Such pilots would soon get the opportunity to get back at the
Hun, just not yet.

On 10 September, 74 Squadron moved to Coltishall which
John found to be an extremely dull and lifeless place. Prior to the
Squadron's arrival, Malan and Stephen were asked to visit 12
Group Headquarters to have an interview with Air Vice Marshal
Trafford Leigh-Mallory to discuss the 'Big Wing': three people in
the same room that John had little time for.

There remained a continuous strain between Freeborn and Malan's relationship for obvious reasons and with H.M. Stephen being so close with Sailor it also caused a few ripples throughout both parties. With the war coming first and foremost, sour feelings didn't necessarily surface but there was certainly an undercurrent between them all, not to mention a few cross words. John's next statement illustrates his own behaviour towards Stephen: 'Mungo, being what he was, a gentle, nice, kindly sort of fellow felt sorry for Stephen and he said to me, "Why are you so nasty to him?" I said "Because I can't bloody stand him and I don't have to like him". There were others who felt the same way'. Despite the apparent dislike for one another, each respected the others ability in the air, and it was this professionalism that made them work as a team and be successful as a Squadron.

As for Leigh-Mallory, John had nothing against him personally, but rather against his approval of the 'Big Wing' concept which he viewed as a 'waste of time'. But whether John agreed with this method or not, he was soon to be a part of it. The 'Big Wing' was conceived by Leigh-Mallory and Squadron Leader Douglas Bader to be a tactic in which three to five squadrons would fly together in formation to meet the enemy *en masse*, with hopes of extinguishing a larger number of raiders than the individual squadrons were achieving on their own. The concept was a controversial subject at the time because Air Vice Marshall Keith Park, who had already experimented with large wings, thought that it was impractical as a defensive tactic for several reasons. One was that getting everybody into position was time consuming. It was thought that by the time the wing got into formation, they would be too late in meeting the raids and another reason, amongst others, was that the pilots had to concentrate so much on staying in position that they didn't have the freedom to search their surroundings for enemy aircraft. The other side to the argument was that simply nibbling at the enemy would not be enough to win the battle. Despite conflicting concerns, the 'Big Wing' was formed at Duxford aerodrome and was to be led by Douglas Bader, flying with 242 Hurricane Squadron.

Malan, although he expressed an interest in the idea, was far more eager to get back into battle after 74 Squadron's three week break and if the 'Big Wing' was his ticket in, then so be it. His one request to Leigh-Mallory during their interview together was that he insisted that 74 Squadron flew at the top, above everyone else.

On 11 September, the Duxford Wing took flight. The poor weather conditions over London proved a small favour for the population of London, who had once again endured a terrifying night of bombing, but their relief was short lived when in the afternoon, as weather conditions improved, the raiders were back. The *Luftwaffe's* tactics had moved from inland airfields to British towns and cities and the fighter boys, more than ever, had their work cut out for them.

In the afternoon heavy raids began to build up over the Pas de Calais and soon enough British shores were visited by large bomber formations accompanied by more than 200 fighter escort. Led by Malan, 74 Squadron flew as rear-guard of three squadrons of the wing. No. 19 Squadron was in front with 611 Squadron at the centre. The Tigers were ordered to intercept the bombers at 20,000 feet while 19 and 611 Squadrons engaged the fighters. Flying in three sections of four in line astern, Malan caught sight of a formation of Ju 88s and ordered an attack. Moments later, his plan was foiled by a gaggle of 109s seen diving in their direction. Turning right across the bombers Malan was able to squirt two of them before evading the 109s. In the chaotic melee of screaming aircraft, Flight Lieutenant Freeborn became separated from his section and unavoidably found he was alone with a Dornier. He made various passes at the bomber, one of which was a head-on attack, undoubtedly killing the crew, for he saw the aircraft fly on with its port engine out, gradually losing height until it finally crashed into a field near Dungeness and burst into flames. As Freeborn swept over the field he noticed a downed He 111 nearby, before climbing back up into the clouds.

Although the 'Big Wing' claimed numerous probables, Freeborn's victory was the only confirmed kill of the sortie. After experiencing the 'Big Wing' concept for himself, John felt that it would be better suited as an offensive tool rather than a defensive one. Fortunately for John, 74 Squadron's involvement with the Duxford Wing was brief.

Some reshuffling took place over the next few days. Stanislaw 'Breezy' Brzezina was given command of the newly formed Polish 308 Squadron, Peter Stevenson was sent to 5 OTU at Aston Down as an instructor and Ernie Mayne left the Tigers with Kelly to become an instructor at 6 OTU. John was sad to see his dear friend of 40 years of age leave the Tigers, but he appreciated that Ernie's talents were needed elsewhere.

During the afternoon of 14 September, Freeborn led Red Section in Spitfire P7368 towards an enemy raid coming in towards Lowestoft. Sergeant Pilot Kirk and Pilot Officer Spurdle were flying as Red Two and Three in his section. After being vectored towards a suspected enemy aircraft, Freeborn's keen blue eyes caught sight of a Heinkel 111K approaching the coast and called, 'Tally-Ho! Turning Port' over the R/T. He dived left and felt his safety straps bite into his shoulders as he went after the invader at 11,000 feet. Closing from about 250 yards to 160, Freeborn fired an accurate three second burst of de Wilde ammunition at the 111, before it escaped into cloud cover. Spurdle was so close to Freeborn at the time that he saw empty cartridge cases pelting out of the vents underneath his leader's wings and towards him. The evading Heinkel re-emerged from its hiding place and Freeborn gave it another burst from close range and silenced the rear-gunner who had been spraying the sky with gun fire. The 111 again hopped into cloud but Spurdle had seen Freeborn's fire clatter the port engine which in turn released white vapour into the air. Both Spurdle and Kirk managed to fire at the 111 as well as Freeborn, so at the end of the patrol they claimed the 111 as a shared aircraft destroyed.

Pilot Officer Bob Spurdle was a New Zealander who gradually began to dislike his Flight Commander as time went on. Freeborn was shaping up to be a fine disciplinarian with his new responsibilities, but such was the nature of the experienced Tigers. Malan was just the same, 'I kick their arses once a day', Sailor said to Tony Bartley on one occasion, '... and I've got a good squadron. Otherwise they'd wind up nothing'. (*Smoke Trails in the Sky.*)

When attacking the He 111 on the 14th one of John's empty cartridges found its way into Spurdles radiator which gave him engine trouble. In Bob Spurdle's book *The Blue Arena* he retells his conversation as Red Three, with Freeborn as Red Leader, like this:

'Hallo, Red Leader, Red Leader. Red Three returning to base, engine trouble, Over'. 'Hallo Windrush, Red Three to Windrush. Please give me vector for base return urgent. Over'.

'Windrush to Red Three, Red Three, steer 260, repeat 260, Over'.

'Red Leader to Red Three. Shut up! Red Leader to Windrush. Any sign of bandit? Over'.

'Hallo, Red Leader. Windrush. Vector 68, five miles, Angels five'.

Understandably, the New Zealander felt hard done by with John's stern response, but it should be remembered that John was an experienced pilot who had a sound understanding of such situations, often being in them himself. In John's mind the R/T needed to be clear in order to prevent a German bomber escaping from their grasp and after all there were plenty of places around for Spurdle to put his aircraft down safely! As it turned out Spurdle limped back to base with his section, feeling thoroughly peeved with his Flight Commander.

In due course Freeborn and Spurdle were again in a similar situation as before but this time pursuing a slippery Messerschmitt 110. John picks up the story:

We intercepted a 110 and we chased the thing all over the sky because it was in and out of cloud. I never really got in a position to shoot it down. I shot at it two or three times but I don't think I hit it . . . in fact I'm sure I didn't! Anyway, we landed and soon after my rigger approached me. He said, 'Have you seen the holes in your aeroplane!?' I said, 'No. It hasn't got any holes in'. My rigger said, 'Well come and have a look then!' So I did, and to my great surprise there were bullet holes all over the place, but the bullets had entered in the wrong direction. They hadn't come from a rear

*gunner, they came from a Spitfire behind me and it was
bloody Spurdle!*

Freeborn stomped back towards the dispersal hut, feeling
thoroughly peeved with his Pilot Officer.

Towards the end of September, the Tigers continued to train
new pilots while the Battle of Britain continued to be waged
heavily further south. The 23rd was a sad occasion for the
Squadron when Sergeant Pilot David Ayers went missing.
During a patrol he was shot down by an unknown enemy aircraft and was seen to evacuate his aircraft over the sea, but on the
4 October his body was washed up onto the shore. Several days
later, tragedy continued to reduce the Tigers' ranks when Pilot
Officer Hastings and Pilot Officer Buckland were tragically
killed in a mid-air collision during a practice formation exercise.
Frank Buckland had been with the Squadron for less than a
week.

Another pilot to arrive with Buckland was Pilot Officer Peter
Chesters. No. 74 weren't to know what had hit them when he
was posted into the Squadron. Chesters was a playful, lovely
character who was undoubtedly terrific for morale during these
dark times. John has many a fond memory of Chesters, which
also brings to mind his partner in crime, Peter St John:

> *The station was a playground for the two Peters. There used
> to be a constant game of poker being played on the beds at
> one end of the room that we used to use. To amuse himself,
> Chester's pulled St John to one side while a heated game of
> poker was being played in the background. Big Peter Chesters
> gave St John his orders. 'Right, when I shout "go", you run
> through the door, jump up on one of the beds and run along
> them all. When you get to the poker school, have a good jump
> there, scatter the cards from the money and then out the exit
> you go'. Not a moment later, Peter St John did exactly what
> Chesters said and ran down the beds sending the game of
> poker into the air. Both Chesters and St John were chased by
> the other pilots who were out for revenge. St John managed
> to get away but Chesters was not so fortunate. He jumped up*

onto the Operations room building and began to walk along a wall trying to escape his pursuers, but he got his footing wrong and slipped off the wall and down into a gap between the operations building and a wooden fence. Chesters was trapped and left at the mercy of his fellow Squadron chums who decided to use the gap below them as a urinal. 'That'll teach you!' they shouted. But it never did.

Peter St John, oh he was a bugger! John says in the nicest possible way. *He was in a different bloody squadron when we were in the air! He wouldn't fly with us, he'd follow us, but he wouldn't fly with us ... but Peter St John, like Chesters, was a likeable villain. The things they used to get up to! One day, I was at our dispersal point and the two Peters turn up, one with a pickaxe and one with a shovel. I said 'What are you two doing now?' And St John said, 'Somewhere just here, a 109 went in and Peter wants to find his luger'. He was bloody luger mad was Chesters. On one occasion the Squadron had been scrambled from Maidstone and Peter Chesters shot a 109 down [it force-landed at Penshurst] and he went in to land to see what he had done to the 109 and gather any souvenirs he could get his hands on, because he was always chasing a luger. Anyway, he landed and the little German pilot [that Chesters put down] didn't like him. He said that Peter hadn't shot him down, but rather he had run out of petrol. Peter called him a bloody liar and they started fighting! Well, Peter was about 6 foot 4 and this German was 5 foot 6 but he was knocking hell out of Peter, so Peter eventually grabbed him and took his Iron Cross off him. The fight was split up when the police arrived and they made Peter hand over the Iron Cross and luger that he had finally obtained. Feeling disappointed with having to hand over his souvenirs, Chesters decided to raid the 109 instead. He pinched a first-aid kit and took off for base, but when he came into land, the first-aid kit fell off his knee and jammed his control stick. Needless to say, his Spitfire ended up on its nose!*

Other than a few brief skirmishes with enemy invaders, 74 Squadron largely missed out on the arduous conflicts fought throughout mid-September and early October. The southern skies were littered with numerous condensation trails made from ferocious dog-fights and aerial activity. The cities, towns and air-fields were left devastated by large raids ruthlessly trying to smash Britain into submission, but the RAF was withstanding the Hun and ruining Hitler's plans.

Illustration by David Pritchard

CHAPTER SIX

Biggin on the Bump

On 15 October 1940, 74 Squadron was sent back to the frontline. John was glad to see the back of Coltishall, but little did he know what was waiting for them in Kent. The Tigers flew in their typical formation over the lovely green fields of southern England and landed together on their new aerodrome, Biggin Hill. The controllers gasped at the sight of a squadron of Spitfires landing in formation because the large, green runway was plagued by bomb craters. Biggin Hill, known as 'Biggin on the bump', was arguably the most frequently attacked airfield throughout the summer campaign. The worst raid to date being on the 30 August when a group of Ju 88s directly hit an air raid shelter, leaving forty airmen and airwomen dead. The *Luftwaffe's* bombs seemed to fall continuously on Biggin, destroying buildings, aircraft, runways and hangers, not to mention personnel and neighbouring civilians. The air was rent with awful sounds of whistling bombs, thunderous explosions, desperate cries and pleas to God. Biggin Hill was in a sorry state and John quickly began to loath the place. The Tigers had been sent to Biggin to replace 72 Squadron, who had been so involved in the fighting of late, that they were reduced to seven pilots over a course of just six weeks. Now, it was 74 Squadron's turn to take the unwieldy reins of Biggin Hill, working alongside 92 Squadron who were also stationed on the bump. No sooner had the Squadron landed and taxied to their new dispersal point than the petrol bowsers began refilling their tanks while ground crewmen started to collect their overnight bags. Moments later, the Spitfires were refuelled and ready to go. As John released the brakes on his Spitfire MK II and began tearing across the grass with the Squadron, he wondered what on earth they were in for at Biggin Hill. He would soon find out.

The Tigers were quartered in a house called Holly Cottage outside the aerodrome's perimeter. They were given a couple of station wagons in order to get the pilots to and from the mess and dispersal point. So far John felt relatively comfortable considering the miserable scene around him. Everywhere he looked maintenance workers could be seen repairing the damage around the station and filling in bomb craters.

One of the first discoveries John and his comrades made at Biggin Hill was that their neighbouring squadron 92 was the complete antithesis of 74 Squadron. No. 92 Squadron was brilliant in the air and had a commendable record amongst their pilots but on the ground they completely lacked discipline and order. They were young men bound by friendship and a desire to enjoy themselves despite the ugly realities of war. Knowing each day might be their last, the boys of 92 behaved accordingly, joking that Sailor Malan was keeping his squadron in order at the point of a pistol. Tony Bartley, an integral member of 92 Squadron made a keen observation of the Tigers in his book *Smoke Trails in the Sky*:

> *No. 74 were fresh compared to us, and started shooting down Huns, right left and centre. Sailor had already become a leading 'ace'. The bulwark of their team consisted of their CO, their flight commanders Mungo-Park and Johnnie Freeborn and Flying Officer Harbourne Mackay Stephen. They were all red hot shots, and the squadron the complete antitheses of 92. They did not indulge themselves in large cars, night clubs or fancy dress.*

Speaking of Malan, Bartley continues:

He considered us just a bunch of playboys, and kept his squadron as distant from ours as possible.

John's assessment of 92 Squadron was just the same. There is no doubt about it, 74 Squadron was built upon a foundation of strong leadership and discipline both on the ground and in the air. Malan even insisted that his pilots should be in bed by 2200 hours, a resolution that would never be entertained in 92 Squadron. In his book *Best of the Few*, Michael Robinson offers an excellent insight into how various pilots of 92 Squadron coped with the situation at Biggin:

Soon after arriving at Biggin Hill, the seriousness of the situation they found themselves in saw several of the pilots give-up smoking, drinking, and late nights. Unfortunately these pilots were the first to be killed, this dispelled any thoughts the others might have of following suit, and if anything, generated an even more cavalier attitude among some of the remaining pilots. Boisterous behaviour, and failure to salute anyone but their own, became their trademark. At one point, Fighter Command was so concerned about 92 they sent some psychologists to study their behaviour. Their conclusion was, 'As long as they continue to perform as well as they do, leave well alone', so the 'fight hard, play hard' theme prevailed ... Drinking for some was the only way to relax quickly, let off steam, and eventually get off to sleep and forget the traumatic events of the day.

During the first few days at Biggin Hill, 74 Squadron was already mixed up in heavy action over Kent. On the 15th they opened their account with Willie Nelson and Peter St John each shooting down a yellow nosed 109. Two days later the Squadron caught the enemy over the Thames Estuary and bagged another three 109s with two probables, but lost Flying Officer Alan

Ricalton, who was suddenly shot down and killed. Ricalton's aircraft crashed at Hollingbourne near Maidstone.

On the 20th, 74 Squadron, accompanied by 66 Squadron caught sight of over thirty Messerschmitt 109s coming south over Maidstone at an altitude of about 29,000 feet. Flight Commanders Freeborn and Mungo Park led the Tigers into action and as usual a dog-fight ensued. Mungo Park's report reads as follows:

> We intercepted a thirty plus raid on Maidstone area at 29,000 feet. The enemy aircraft were slightly below us and we dived from 500 feet above. They immediately dived away and then half of them zoomed up. I followed them up and fired a short burst of four seconds at the rear machine. He immediately spun and I followed him down to about 4,000 feet, when his tail unit broke away. I had to break off the engagement as I was being fired at from behind, and do not know whether the pilot baled out.

H.M. Stephen flying as Mungo Park's number two also destroyed a 109 when he pounced onto a section of four that dived towards Dungeness. When they got down to 9,000 feet, Stephen engaged the 109 on the far left of the section and watched his ammunition chew into the tail and the cockpit area of the aircraft. He watched the cockpit hood fly off the Messerschmitt before breaking away from the other three climbing towards him. He managed to evade their guns before latching onto another 109. After a six second burst, Stephen watched the German pilot bale out of his aircraft which ended up crashing into a nearby wood.

Another Tiger to put a 109 into the ground was Pilot Officer Ben Draper before his radiator sustained damage and he was forced to crash land his aircraft. Draper walked away unscathed but two of the Squadron's Sergeant Pilots were not as lucky. Clive Hilken was shot down in the ruckus but managed to bale out of his Spitfire, wounded. He was later admitted to Orpington War Hospital. Sergeant Thomas Kirk was also shot down by a 109 and baled out with grievous injuries. John went to see

Thomas in hospital and was able to record the following report before Thomas died:

> I, Sergeant Kirk, was followed by P/O Draper, who was Yellow three. I was Yellow four. P/O Draper attacked one Me 109, and I attacked another. The enemy aircraft dived and I followed. Large pieces of the enemy aircraft fell off the fuselage and wings. The end of the enemy aircraft's dive was unobserved, as I was attacked and shot down.

On Tuesday the 22nd, nine Spitfires led by Malan took flight to intercept single enemy raiders, but no contact was made. They were soon instructed to join 92 Squadron, who were patrolling at 30,000 feet over Ashford. Shortly after 1400 hours, they spotted six 109s below at 26,000 feet and engaged. Malan dived after one of the bandits firing a couple of bursts from 200 yards which caused the 109 to puff smoke before it levelled out at 8,000 feet and made for the coast. Malan decided to break away from the attack due to ice build up on his windscreen. As it turned out the German pilot was forced to bale out into the sea, where he was rescued and taken prisoner. Mungo Park also downed a 109 but the Germans got their reprisal.

Bob Spurdle was forced to evacuate his Spitfire after chasing a 109 down in a dive from 27,000 feet. He picked up so much speed in the dive that his aircraft began to judder violently and then whip round in a spin. The starboard wing was torn right off the aircraft sending Spurdle spiralling towards the earth before he managed to force the cockpit hood back and vacate his aircraft. While he floated down in his parachute he froze as cannonfire whizzed past him followed by a venomous 109E. As the 109 climbed in front of Spurdle, preparing for another pass, he wriggled frantically in his harness feeling terrified. Suddenly two Spitfires flown by Stephen and Churches roared onto the scene and scared the 109 into a half roll. Stephen managed to chase it guns blazing leaving Spurdle to float down towards a field without further threat.

Despite the friction between Freeborn and Spurdle, John was angry when he learned of the German's behaviour towards a

helpless airmen dangling from a parachute. After this occurrence John would occasionally squirt some ammunition above
German aircrew that were descending in their parachutes, much
to Stephen's annoyance. Never did he hit a parachute nor did he
intend to, but when John thought of his family cowering in an
air raid shelter or the poor civilians of Kent being strafed by
machine guns while they worked in their fields, he felt a slight
sensation of payback. This is not to say that all *Luftwaffe* pilots
behaved this way, for many of them were simply doing their
duty, just like the British, but John admits that there were
undoubtedly some 'bad apples' amongst the German ranks.

The loss of Spurdle's Spitfire was the least of 74 Squadron's
worries. Peter St John was dead. It was heart-rending for the
Squadron, especially for those like John and Chesters who were
particularly close to him. The circumstances surrounding his
death were unknown to the Squadron, although John expects he
was probably bounced by a 109. The hardest part about the war
was losing friends and fellow pilots. One day they were in the
Mess carrying on as normal and then suddenly they were gone,
never to return. It was a hard process to swallow because it hurt
and it was saddening, but then it had to be put away in order
for morale to shine through. A pilot didn't have time to dwell
on death, or on the possibility that next time it might be them,
because if they did it probably would be.

John remarks that his time on the bump was wretched. 'I never
liked Biggin Hill, even to this day. I remember one awful day in
particular. We just had a runway built and we were sitting in the
dispersal hut talking and suddenly there's a whoosh! An 88
came right over at low level and dropped bombs all the way
down the new runway and disappeared. There was no way we
could catch it. I thought he was a brave guy for doing that, but it
was a loathsome time'.

In spite of the depressing weeks at Biggin Hill, the boys still
managed to find ways to amuse themselves. Once a week they
would be released from flying duty and would gather up all the
12 bore rifles that they could get their hands on and go pheasant
shooting. John knew where there were some pheasants because
he'd seen them in a garden when he was flying one day. So off the

boys went one afternoon with their 12 bores and started shooting some pheasants that were penned in. They then volunteered Mungo Park to climb over the fence and gather up the birds that they had shot. As Mungo was chucking the dead pheasants over the fence, the game keeper came along and caught him redhanded. 'What do you think you're doing!?' He asked the embarrassed fighter pilot. 'Oh, we just wanted a pheasant, if the owner wouldn't mind?' Mungo replied. 'Do you know who the owner is?' Mungo looked at his comrades sniggering on the other side of the fence before answering. 'No, but I'm sure he's wealthy enough to have a gamekeeper and a pen like this'. As the gamekeeper spoke the pilots on the other side of the fence stopped their antics and Mungo gulped. 'His name is Winston Churchill. So I'll be having your name!' 'Don't tell him Mungo! Don't tell him your name!' Peter St John shouted over the fence, 'Archbishop of Canterbury will do Mungo!' Luckily for Mungo he was soon let out of the gate but the gamekeeper asked for the pheasants back. 'Sod off', John shouted as they made a run for it with their game. The boys took their lovely pheasants to a local pub where the landlady cooked them and it 'was a jolly good meal'.

Sunday 27 October, was another busy day for 74 Squadron. On the first morning patrol, Flying Officer Nelson, flying as Malan's No. 2 destroyed a 109 which crashed near Rochford aerodrome. Shortly after, 'A' Flight fought their way through the cloudy weather and towards another sweep of 109s at approximately 23,000 feet. In the resulting dog-fight over Maidstone, gun covers were quickly torn away by Spitfire ammunition. H.M. Stephen watched a 109 he had been attacking burst into flames after closing to about 200 yards. Mungo Park, fronting 'B' Flight, managed to damage another 109 with just one gun, the others, he soon discovered, had frozen. Bill Skinner latched onto another fighter and gave it a decent burst before it dived steeply towards the sea trailing black smoke. This was the same day that Peter Chesters took his 109 down to Penshurst to 'capture his prisoner'. His report reads:

> *The enemy which I attacked was diving down to the clouds and I followed him. He saw me and tried to get on to my tail. I*

managed to turn inside him and put a burst into his engine,
causing it to stop. I jockeyed him earthwards, and he landed
on Penshurst Aerodrome with his wheels in the up position. I
landed on the same aerodrome.

The day did not conclude with a happy ending, for Sergeant Pilot J.A. Scott, a newcomer to the Squadron, was killed in action.

The following patrols leading up to the end of the month were spent scrapping with Messerschmitt 109s, where the Tigers again proved themselves to be efficient marksmen in the air.

The 31 October 1940, brought drizzly rain upon the south of England in a feeble attempt to cleanse the air of blood. The Battle of Britain was over in as much as the *Luftwaffe* had failed to gain air superiority over the RAF. Nevertheless, their attacks, although weakened, continued to harass the British and Fighter Command in the months to follow. John Freeborn, who had flown more operational hours during this intense period of conflict than anyone else, was surely due a rest.

November opened with another loss for 74 Squadron. Flying Officer Nelson was reported missing and Sergeant Pilot Soars was wounded and admitted to the Victoria Hospital in Folkestone. It was later learnt that the American, Willie Nelson, had been killed in action.

On 2 November, 74 Squadron received orders to patrol Biggin Hill with 92 Squadron at 0811 hours. Sailor Malan led the Tigers up to 30,000 feet flying alongside Johnny Kent leading 92 Squadron. Due to the cold air, Johnny Kent took them down to a lower altitude because their aircraft were leaving vapour trails; a dead giveaway of their position. The Tigers were soon vectored towards Maidstone where they were to find approximately sixty Bf 109s flying in open formation at 20,000 feet. The Spitfires engaged over the Isle of Sheppey and enemy aircraft began to fall. Pilot Officer Churches put a good burst into a 109 and sent it vertically into the sea, Mungo Park managed to draw white smoke from another's engine before breaking off due to an iced up windscreen, Sergeant Skinner sent one down in flames and Pilot Officer Spurdle put one down in a field outside Ashford.

The boys of 92 Squadron also fared well during the scrap. Bob Holland sent a 109 bouncing across the waves, Johnny Kent destroyed two 109s with an additional probable, Bill Watling destroyed a 109 and Geoffrey Wellum damaged a further two.

Good news arrived for two of the Tigers on the 5th. Mungo Park was awarded the DFC and the Scotsman, H.M. Stephen, was awarded a bar to his DFC.

The next significant day for the Squadron was nine days later, when both John and Malan were finally away on leave. In Sailor's absence, Mungo Park led the Squadron. At 1345 hours, 74 took off from Biggin Hill with 66 Squadron with orders to patrol the aerodrome at 15,000 feet. For a while the Spitfires circled around the station like protective birds of prey until suddenly they were ordered to Deal to patrol at 18,000 feet. Soon enough the thumping of Ack-Ack fire boomed into the air at a large formation of enemy aircraft approaching Dover from the north-east. The fighter boys zoomed into action with their gun buttons set to 'fire'. The enemy raid consisted of about fifty Ju 87 Stukas formed up in tight vics of five, flying in line astern at 12,000 feet. Mungo Park led the Tigers to engage, ever mindful of the twenty-five Bf 109s flying as top cover. After firing a three-second burst at close range, Mungo watched his ammunition strike the dive bomber before it burst into flames. H.M. Stephen was next to get in on the act. He swooped down upon a section of three Ju 87s and gave one of them a five-second burst of gun fire. The Junkers rolled and smashed straight into the aircraft flying adjacent to it. Stephen engaged a third and sent it towards the Channel in flames. The melee was frantic and the Stukas were hopelessly outclassed. Walter Franklin also set a Junkers ablaze during the engagement. Not forgetting the 109s, Wally Churches spent some difficult moments evading their attacks until at 16,000 feet he locked-on to a lone Messerschmitt caught unaware. Churches thumbed the gun button for four seconds which caused the 109 to cough thick black smoke. Bits and pieces fell of its wings before it rolled lazily onto its back and descended in flames. Ben Draper was having the fight of his life as he peppered a Ju 87 with a well timed deflection shot. The Ju 87 began to fall apart as it plunged vertically towards the deck. Fastening on to a second, Draper fired a short burst and put another 87 down in flames. Draper's battle was not yet over. He lined up yet another Junkers in his gun sight and shot it into the sea below and then expended the remainder of his ammunition into a 109, which managed to get away with slight damage. Another Tiger to claim three Ju 87s destroyed was a Sergeant Pilot by the name of John Glendinning. The Sergeant Pilot made two head-on attacks during the interception and put one Ju 87 down in flames and another streaming dark smoke. The third Junkers to be destroyed by his guns went down with pieces falling off its wings. One of the new replacement pilots, Bill Armstrong, destroyed a Stuka before being hit by a cannon shell which put his aircraft in flames. Being burnt by fire was every pilot's worst nightmare, but luckily Armstrong quickly baled out of his Spitfire and landed safely near Worth. Others to score against the enemy were Bob Spurdle, Bill Skinner and Laurence Freese. It had been a highly successful engagement for 74 Squadron who ended the day with fifteen confirmed enemy aircraft destroyed, two probables and several others damaged. Malan was sick that he had missed the interception. He sent a telegram to the Tigers simply saying 'Congratulations you rats – Sailor'. Had Freeborn and Malan participated in this action, there is no doubt that 74's tally would have been increased.

On 17 November, John Freeborn was back in the air with eleven other Tigers patrolling the Rochford line at around 1515 hours. The Tigers climbed to 15,000 feet with 92 Squadron leading. As per usual, the squadrons were directed to various positions. No. 92 Squadron was vectored towards Eastbourne, while 74 Squadron turned away for Littlehampton to fend off some thirty plus enemy aircraft that had been sighted. On arriving, the Tigers began to sweep the area from a westerly course along the coast and soon discovered vapour trails above them heading in a northerly direction. The Squadron began to climb towards the vapour trails but broke off as they were bounced by twenty Bf 109s flying in pairs. Needless to say, a dog-fight erupted in the sky causing aircraft to twist, turn, climb and dive in all directions. Freeborn flying Spitfire II P7542 put his throttle 'through the gate' and fired at the leading 109 but to no avail. He then turned his attention to another 109 in the formation and opened up his eight machine guns. Each gun flashed brightly from the wings and pelted ammunition at the same 109 H.M. Stephen was attacking. Practically elbowing each other out of the way, the two pilots continued their attacks as the 109 dived in an attempt to throw off its pursuers. Freeborn and Stephen closed in on the German fighter and gave it another couple of bursts. Unable to cope with the joint attack, the 109 crashed into the sea near Brighton. Freeborn and Stephen pulled back on their control columns and climbed rapidly away for Biggin Hill.

John's report for this engagement reads:

> I was leading 74 Squadron on patrol when we intercepted appox 15 to 20 Me 109s. I attacked leading E/A and did not observe any result. I then attacked No. 3 of E/A Formation. It then dived and I followed it down, I gave two bursts and a faint trail of smoke came out of the engine. I gave one more burst and the E/A crashed into sea. Yellow Leader also attacked E/A.

The deteriorating weather meant that there was less aerial activity during the following week, a welcomed relief for some.

On 27th, while patrolling at 25,000 feet above the Isle of Sheppey, Anti Aircraft fire began to pound into the sky at enemy raiders. Malan led the Tigers towards the A.A. bursts to investigate and immediately spotted two Bf 109s flying south at about 30,000 feet. The Squadron gave chase and before the 109s dived towards the haze below, a German voice was heard over the R/T yelling 'Achtung, Spitfire!' Malan lost sight of the 109s after firing an inaccurate burst but caught them again at 5,000 feet over Dungeness where he shot one of them down from a range of 150 yards closing to 50 yards. The 109 began to break apart on its way down to the sea. The second 109 was also hit and smoking badly when Squadron Leader H.J. Wilson, on detachment from the Royal Aircraft Establishment at Farnborough in Hampshire, to gain combat experience, finished it off.

At around the same time as Malan's interception, Peter
Chesters was to be found over Chatham where he was bounced
by an enemy aircraft he hadn't seen. The attack left his controls
badly damaged and his leg searing with pain. Even though his
Spitfire was severely damaged, Chesters managed to steer it
away from a village and towards the mudflats of Conyer Creek
where he baled out. Still in agony from his leg injury, the pilot
landed relatively safely and was swiftly rescued by a local Air
Raid Warden. As Chesters recovered in hospital, an unsigned
letter was sent to Biggin Hill's CO. It read:

> *I and the people of a small village in north-east Kent would
> very much like to thank the pilot of a fighter plane who baled
> out over some marshes for staying at his controls and steering
> his damaged plane away from the village and a factory before
> baling out.*

Peter's bravery was warmly appreciated by the Kentish
people, who were rightly saved from a falling Spitfire. Now, the
wounded pilot was able to rest from his labours for a time, but
that didn't keep him out of mischief, as John remembers.

> *My life was full of getting into trouble, or getting Chesters
> and St John out of trouble. They lived on it. When Peter
> Chesters was shot down by a German, he caught a bullet in the
> leg that went down his shin and through his ankle. Walter
> Franklin was getting married at this time in Maidenhead
> and Peter was the best man. He was pretty badly wounded
> but Franklin asked the matron if he could be released from
> hospital because Peter was his best man. She said 'Yes, but
> you better take care of him and no messing about!' So we put
> him in the car and off we went to Maidenhead via a lot of
> pubs. We could barely pass a pub without going in. So there
> we were going down the North Camp road and we stop
> at some traffic lights where there's a bobby on horseback.
> Peter said to me, 'When the traffic lights change, get your
> foot down and go'. I said, 'Why?' and Peter said, 'Because I
> told you so!' He wound the window down and the next thing*

I know he's got his walking stick out. The lights change and he's shouting 'Go!' and he put the stick straight over the police horse's arse and it flew up in the air and chucked the bobby off and we were gone. I thought 'Oh it's going to be one of those days', and it bloody was. Poor Franklin kept moaning as we made our way to the church. 'I'm getting married at 3 o'clock' and Peter would say 'Well it's only 2:30 by my watch and it might be a bit fast'. So we'd have another drink. We eventually got to the church and Peter staggered in, sat down in a pew, put his feet up and lit a fag. The next thing I remember is being thrown out into the street. The bride's family came out and said to Franklin, 'Are you in charge of these hooligans?' and he said, 'No, they're in charge of me. I have to do what I'm told with this lot!' We were called everything that was bad, and I think I agree with them, we were.

John and Peter were promptly told that they were not invited to the reception but after John retrieved some of Churchill's pheasants from the boot of his car, the bride's mother soon came around.

Towards the end of the month, 66, 74 and 92 Squadron had an incredible record of destroyed enemy aircraft between them. On the 29 November, the tally at Biggin Hill stood at 599 kills. A sweepstake swiftly went around the station as bets were placed on whom would get the 600th kill and when. The pilot who achieved the 600th kill would be rewarded by the kitty. The following day, the takings would be won.

The 30th dawned cold and cloudy. A low mist covered the aerodrome putting many of the pilots at ease. Flying certainly seemed off as far as the morning weather was concerned. Then out of nowhere the serene atmosphere of the aerodrome was broken by the sound of two Merlin Spitfire engines roaring down the runway at Biggin Hill. The noise caught the attention of those around the station, who all took a keen interest into finding out which two pilots were mad enough to take off in such poor conditions. 'Of all the bloody cheek!' remarked the Station Commander when he learnt it was Mungo Park and H.M.

Stephen. A bunch of cars and motor bicycles led by Malan
screamed off towards the Operations Room to follow the boys
over the R/T. The two pilots called the Controller informing him
that they were out on a voluntary patrol to which 11 Group
responded, 'Vector those two idiots to Deal. There's a convoy
moving up-Channel which might tempt Jerry – even in this
weather!' As the two Spitfire pilots broke through the haze they
entered a clear patch of sky where they spotted eight Bf 109s
at around 30,000 feet. Mungo Park and Stephen climbed to
34,000 feet and engaged the formation, selecting the 'Weaver' as
their target. Mungo was the first to press the gun button giving
the 109 a two-second burst before it took evasive action and
dived. Mungo was at such a distance that he broke off from the
attack for fear of overshooting the Messerschmitt which allowed
Stephen to follow up the attack. The 109 half-rolled and Mungo
followed it down firing another short burst at 100 yards and
closing. Again, Mungo broke away from the attack to avoid the
109's hood that had flung off towards him. Stephen got into
position and released his ammunition. The last Mungo saw of
the 109 was it going down through cloud in a vertical position.
The 109 crashed near Dungeness and the German pilot died
fifteen hours later. He was thereafter buried with full military
honours.

The 600th kill had made Biggin Hill the first station in Fighter
Command to reach such a figure. The credit however, was
awarded to H.M. Stephen, despite the fact that Mungo Park,
according to John, was the one to shoot it down. John recalls
that Mungo was far too much of a gentleman to say anything
different at the time, and that Malan's influence swayed the claim
to his pal Stephen. John is adamant that Stephen had arranged
for the Controllers to tip him off before hand, so that he could get
a head start in claiming the 600th victory for the station. When
the call eventually came through, Stephen was ready to go and
Mungo, who was present at the time, was detailed to go with
him. Some accounts of this story state that the kitty was equally
divided between both pilots, but John remembers otherwise.

Leaving aside the suspect claim, 74 Squadron was nevertheless, a force to be reckoned with. According to 11 Group

Headquarters, the boys had chalked up twenty-six enemy aircraft destroyed for the month of November.

As December opened the Tigers kept up the pace. Henryk
Szczesny and Malan shared a Bf 109 on the 1st and the following
day they each got another. Other pilots to join the combat reports
for the 2nd were Neil Morrison and John Glendinning who also
downed a 109 apiece. John's time would come just three days
later.

On Thursday 5 December, twelve Spitfires of 74 Squadron
arose in formation from the grassy aerodrome at Biggin Hill and
followed 92 Squadron on an afternoon sortie. Allan Wright, a
quiet, mild mannered fighter pilot of 92, led the patrol towards
Canterbury, flying a cannon armed Spitfire. After thirty minutes
into the trip, Wright handed over leadership to Tony Bartley
due to R/T failure. Shortly after, 92 Squadron received orders to
climb to 30,000 feet but they settled at 20,000 to avoid a high
layer of cloud. 92, bearing the Squadron code 'QJ', then made
their way towards Dover where A.A. guns were thumping in
anger. Curiously enough, John Freeborn found himself in the
same predicament as Wright. His combat report explains:

> I was leading the Squadron on a patrol following No. 92
> Squadron. As my R/T packed up I took over Yellow Section
> and Yellow Leader led the Squadron. Just after the change-
> over we sighted six Me 109s.

Instinctively 'pulling the plug' Freeborn went full throttle
towards the 109s and picked out the leader, giving it a one-
second deflection burst at about 50 yards. The 109 dived and
Freeborn followed, squirting it with a two-second burst of
ammunition at a closing range of 150 to 100 yards. The second
attack was too much to handle for the German machine and it
crashed into the sea ten to fifteen miles off Dungeness. Freeborn
climbed back towards the coast with his sharp blue eyes searching his surroundings for any 'Snappers'. With a dry mouth and
sweaty palms, Freeborn latched on to another 109 and attacked
it from astern. With the enemy in sight, he pressed the tit on his
control stick and sunk his bullets into the 109's cooling system.

Then, out of nowhere a 92 Squadron, cannon equipped Spitfire, peppered the aircraft with shells and sent it crashing into the sea with an almighty splash.

John's combat report continues:

> *I then met another Me 109 and did two deflection attacks from above, giving two, two-second bursts. The E/A set on fire and crashed into the sea 10 miles off Boulogne. I then saw several more Me 109s returning to France and one was well behind the formation. I did an astern attack and finished all my ammunition. Pieces of fuselage fell off this enemy aircraft.*

According to John's report, he had fired a total of 2,700 rounds during this engagement, claiming two Bf 109s destroyed, one shared and one damaged. Not a bad day's work!

On 12 December, 'Henry the Pole' Szczeney was posted from 74 to join Bob Standford Tuck's 257 Squadron. The following day, more awards were handed out to the Tigers. Malan was awarded the Distinguished Service Order, H.M. Stephen received the DSO, Ben Draper the DFC and Bill Skinner was awarded the DFM. The Squadron continued to flourish and by the end of 1940, 74 Squadron's official tally stood at 124 confirmed victories and 47 damaged for the loss of 11 pilots to enemy action.

CHAPTER SEVEN

A New Year

The Battle for Britain had been won and the threat of a German invasion upon England was reduced. At the beginning of the New Year, the RAF turned its attention away from defensive patrols and towards offensive sweeps over France, with hopes of drawing enemy fighters into the air. The following months, although busy for the fighter and bomber boys, were in no way as desperate for Britain as the previous summer and autumn of 1940 had been, although bombing raids on a lesser and infrequent scale were to continue, usually at night. After an exhausting period for the pilots on either side of the Channel, times were now changing, and the *Luftwaffe* was now facing the sharp end of the RAF's arsenal.

The first couple of months saw 74 Squadron flying across the Channel with 92 and 66 Squadron conducting fighter Sweeps and Circus sorties over the French coast. By now, H.M. Stephen had left the Tigers, having been posted to RAF Turnhouse. In early January the Squadron suffered another loss to their ranks, when Lawrence Freece fatally force-landed at Detling, after running out of fuel.

On 5 February 1941, Control requested that two sections of 74 Squadron should be sent up to investigate hostile activity over Dover. Malan took off with Red Section and Freeborn took off

leading Yellow Section. As the two sections of 'ZP' Spitfires
approached Dover at 10,000 feet, they received further information regarding an enemy bandit approaching the English coast
between Dover and Folkestone at low altitude. Red Section
dived through a large layer of cloud, with Yellow Section
following. As Red Section broke through the cloud base, they
quickly caught sight of a Dornier 215 turning south off Dover at
about 2,000 feet. The 'Tally Ho!' was called by Red Leader and
the Tigers pressed on to attack the lone bomber. Malan noticed
that the bomber seemed unusually slow and marvelled that the
pilot took no evasive action to avoid their attack. Approaching
the Dornier from slightly below, Sailor Malan opened fire
at around 150 yards and hit the 215's engines and fuselage,
while the rear gunner returned fire. Malan's Spitfire was struck
in the spinner and mainplane area by the German gunner, so he
manoeuvred out of harm's way before returning for a second
attack from dead astern. Malan's Red Two, Flying Officer Bill
Armstrong also positioned himself to attack and awoke his
machine guns from about 300 yards range with a two second
burst, then at 250 yards he thumbed his gun button for a further
six seconds before breaking off due to the rear gunner's persist-
ence. An explosion erupted from under the Dornier's port engine
and a thick cloud of oil sprayed out onto Red Two's windscreen,
forcing him to break away. Presumably, the enemy aircraft had
been fully equipped with state of the art armour plating because
it even put up with a third attack from Malan's eight machine
guns which finally fell silent. Malan broke off, with Armstrong
formatting on his leader's wing and Yellow Section continued
the attack. Flight Lieutenant Freeborn screamed into a beam
attack from the left and Pilot Officer Peter Chesters made a
pass from the right. Following a second burst, Freeborn saw the
Dornier's port engine blow up and noticed that the rear gunner
had been silenced. The Dornier was now flying just a couple of
hundred feet above the sea. Freeborn and Chesters continued to
spray it with their Browning machine guns and then suddenly,
Chesters watched one of the German crew members climb out
of the aircraft onto the port wing and drop off into the sea just

as the Dornier collided with the water, letting off an enormous silvery-white spray.

Between the four pilots who attacked the Dornier, they had fired 6,541 rounds. John, flying Spitfire P7366 at the time, accounted for 1,360 of them.

On 17 February, John Freeborn learnt that he had been awarded a bar to his DFC. By this time, the young man from Yorkshire had flown continuous operational sorties with distinction. He had led the Squadron and his section on numerous occasions over the previous months and had proven himself to be a prolific fighter pilot in the air. At the time he was awarded a bar to his DFC, John had destroyed twelve enemy aircraft and damaged many more.

Shortly after John received the good news, 74 Squadron moved to Manston for a brief spell. It was from here Pilot Officer Wally Churches and Sergeant Pilot Neil Morrison destroyed a Messerschmitt 110. Two days later, Morrison was reported missing and Sergeant Pilot Jan Rogowski crash-landed near Eastbourne where he was admitted to hospital with head injuries. Rogowski was a well liked Pole who had previously served with 303 Squadron during the Battle of Britain before joining the Tigers on 7 February, after being sent from 91 Squadron. As a Polish pilot, he certainly lived up to 303's reputation, by being aggressive and passionate in the sky.

A change was in the air as March dawned. Sailor Malan left 74 Squadron after four years and two months of service, becoming the Biggin Hill Wing Leader, which meant that he would still be leading the Tigers in some respect, along with 92 and 609 Squadrons in Fighter Wing offensives. As a result of Malan's departure, John Mungo Park was promoted to lead 74 Squadron. Mungo's new position came as a surprise for some, including John, who felt that he was not necessarily the right choice for the job. As much as John liked and respected Mungo, he couldn't help but feel that this was another screening effort orchestrated by Malan. After all, John had led the Squadron on countless occasions, gaining irreplaceable experience and yet he was never considered for the position. This is not to say that John would have welcomed the promotion anyway, because at this stage

John 'had had a belly full of flying and non-stop operations since the beginning of the war' and would have found it a taxing responsibility to bear. Other Tigers like Bob Spurdle for example, found Mungo's promotion to be a relief.

To fill the gap, Malan offered Mungo's previous position to Tony Bartley, who was still with 92 Squadron at the time. The next day Bartley accepted the offer and thereafter became A Flight Commander in 74 Squadron, after promising Sailor that he would turn over a new leaf.

As the spring weather arrived, the Tigers continued to shoot down enemy aircraft throughout March and April. On 4 March, John shared a Dornier 17 with Pilot Officer Bob Poulton. On the 18th, Churches downed a 109, as did Rogowski and Pilot Officer Howard on 7 April. Three days later tragedy struck the Squadron.

After shooting down a Bf 109 over Manston, Peter Chesters darted across the aerodrome at low altitude and attempted a victory roll to celebrate his success. John looked on in horror as he watched Peter's Spitfire stall, flick roll, and plunge straight into the ground. Seeing a close friend killed like this, after surviving months of fearsome dog fights, was absolutely devastating. 'Poor old Peter. I remember him being on night-flying duty, so he had to fly his aeroplane during the day to test it. During his test flight two 109s flew over Manston and Peter chased them and put one of them down. He came back and did the most unforgivable thing. He did a roll over the aerodrome at bugger all speed. It was so slow it turned into a flick roll and he went straight into the ground. That was one of the saddest periods of our time. I was very fond of Peter. He was a crack shot and a very good pilot'.

Over a week later, Wally Churches was also lost to the Squadron. Wally was a gentle soul; his loss was felt strongly by the Tigers.

In May, 74 Squadron moved to Gravesend and began to be re-equipped with Spitfire MK Vs. The new Marks were armed with two 20mm cannons and four .303 machine guns. The overall performance was an improvement from the previous models of Spitfire, nevertheless, John felt more comfortable in the Mark II.

On 6 June, twenty-one year old John Freeborn gathered up his belongings and left 74 Squadron. The top brass had decided that he had spent enough time on the front line and was due a rest. That is not to say that he wasn't kept busy in the following months, for his talents were put to good use at 57 Operation Training Unit, Hawarden.

Reflecting upon his departure from the Tigers John remarks:

> *It was war time. We didn't enjoy the war but we fought it to the best of our ability and we were very good at it. I was relieved to be away from the fighting. 74 Squadron was one of the best fighter squadrons in the air force, I was glad to be a member of it and I did what I had to do.*

October 1938, seemed a lifetime ago for John. He began as a fresh-faced, inexperienced young man, wandering around Hornchurch trying to adjust to squadron life, while keenly watching the older pilots around him. Now, he was a Spitfire ace that had endured the awful ordeal of Barking Creek, Dunkirk and the Battle of Britain. In just a few years, John had experienced more than most people ever will in a lifetime. He had watched enemy aircraft fall at the touch of a button, he had seen many close friends and acquaintances die in their youth. The loss of Don Cobden, Peter St John, Peter Chesters, Wally Churches, Ben Draper, Tony Mould, Peter Stevenson, Willie Nelson, John Mungo Park and many others, undoubtedly left a lasting impression on young Freeborn. The discipline and lessons learnt in 74 Squadron, both in the air and on the ground, would never be forgotten.

57 OTU at Hawarden was located just south of Chester. John's general responsibility as an instructor was to convert pilots who had initially trained in Canada to the Spitfire. Naturally, the rookies didn't just climb straight into a Spitfire cockpit on arrival, some of them hadn't flown for a year, so a refresher course on the Magister came first and foremost. The process was almost as stressful as being on the front line! John soon became accustomed to pilots getting lost, landing at different airfields, landing on their bellies and more seriously, crashing their aircraft.

It was certainly a new experience for John, but one he quickly adapted to. The days were often long and hard work for the instructors at Hawarden, but John, ever the skirt chaser, found the energy to keep the local girls entertained. John well remembers several girls asking him for a ride in an aeroplane, as they watched from the airfield's perimeter. Not wanting to disappoint, John, on several occasions met their needs and took them up in a Magister, mainly at Wrexham due to the lack of security. On one occasion when John was enjoying a pleasant trip with a young lady he asked her if she could see her house. The excited girl looked over the side and after a few moments replied that she couldn't. That was a big mistake! John rolled the aircraft so that they were inverted and shouted over her screams, 'How about now?' Putting the Magister through its paces when accompanied by naive females never got old for the fighter pilot.

John looks back at his time away from the front line with fondness, because for just a short while, he was able to appreciate the pleasures in life that most young men today are free to enjoy, pleasures they possibly take for granted. However, the nights out on the town and his many adventures with the opposite sex almost came to an abrupt end, as Squadron Leader Tony Pickering explains in his recollections of John:

> I know that John Freeborn was a regular Royal Air Force Officer with 74 Squadron before the 1939–45 war, but I came in contact with him when he was a Flight Commander with 74 Squadron at Biggin Hill in September to October 1940. The contact was somewhat vague as I was a humble Sergeant Pilot with 501 Squadron at Gravesend and Kenley. We flew as a Wing at times with 74, when the Huns were bombing our airfields, docks etc, and would hear the chatter on the R/T between the Squadron. John, flying under Sailor Malan as CO was well respected as a senior Flight Commander. He and Sailor Malan were the most successful pilots in 74 Squadron. I later met up with John when he commanded a Flight at 57 OTU at Hawarden, 1941. I was still a Sergeant Pilot, but later in 1941 received my commission as a Pilot Officer. John was a very strict disciplinarian, and his pupils who were

learning to fly Spitfires respected his firm instructions, sometimes harsh, but in my opinion no doubt saved the lives of these young pilots. I could mention the 'Stocks' which John set up to punish the young pilots who misbehaved and which John was told to remove, but that is an entirely different story.

In Tony's log book he has recorded a flight he had with John in a Tiger Moth, dated 16 June 1941. Tony continues:

I must have delivered a Spitfire [to Wrexham] and picked up a Tiger Moth to fly back to Hawarden and was told to take John Freeborn back to Hawarden. I do remember the short trip well, as due to a misunderstanding it was very nearly our last flight! He asked if he could take over to do some aerobatics, or probably told me, and after ten minutes of his demonstration, he handed back the aircraft to me, but I did not hear him, and the aircraft flew for five minutes without a pilot.

When the Tiger Moth began to descend to tree level, John grabbed the controls and climbed back to safety. Fortunately, the two pilots returned to Hawarden without further trouble. Today, both John and Tony laugh when talking about this incident, although one is confident that neither of them found it amusing at the time!

In December 1941, John Freeborn's time with 57 OTU came to an end and shortly after, he was posted to the United States of America as a Liaison Officer. As John sailed across the Atlantic Ocean in the 25,000 ton SS *Rangitiki*, a new adventure was beginning for the young man from Headingley. The long days of dawn readiness, strenuous dog fighting and continuous interceptions over the Channel were now over for John, but his future in the RAF did not come without the dangers of escort patrols and sea and land attack sorties. Throughout the following years John would serve in 602 Squadron as a Squadron Leader supernumerary, then onto 118 Squadron as Commanding Officer and then finally, John became the RAF's youngest Wing Commander, responsible for the 286 Italian Wing stationed at Grottaglie.

It was in 1946 that Wing Commander John Connell Freeborn DFC and Bar left the Royal Air Force with honour and distinction. It had been a long and tiring journey, which had shaped a young boy of eighteen years old, into a confident, capable man with ample of experience under his belt. John had learnt a vast amount of lessons during his RAF service, many of which have stayed with him until this very day.

There is no doubt that John Freeborn had been through a lot in his young life. He had made it through the tumultuous episode of Barking Creek, endured the Battle of Britain and success-fully commanded the largest wing in Italy. John's example of courage and perseverance in those trying days are nothing short of inspiring and such is the reason behind the telling of his remarkable story.

Illustration by David Pritchard

Epilogue

I n 2007 I stood with Wing Commander John Freeborn on the edge of Manston's airfield and watched a commercial jet take off into the blue summer sky. 'I bet this looks different from when you were last here John', I said, looking into the wise old face of the Yorkshireman. 'Totally different', John replied casting his eyes across Manston. Little did I know that a year later I would be writing about John Freeborn as a young pilot in 74 Squadron, who regularly took off in a Spitfire from the very same aerodrome we were standing on, to intercept multitudes of enemy aircraft.

I have spent a considerable amount of time with John over the last few years, both socially and at different aviation signing events and air shows, where he refers to me as his 'batman'. I have thoroughly enjoyed the many hours we have spent together discussing a wide range of subjects, but generally his war experiences during 1940. I have grown enormously fond of John and therefore was struck by an unquenchable desire to pay tribute to the wonderful man and friend that he is by writing this book.

From the very beginning I made the decision to concentrate solely on John's time with 74 Squadron because it was with the Tigers that he experienced the most unforgettable and intense moments of his life, which in a practical sense meant that such memories and research were more readily accessible for us both. This book does not claim to be a biographical account of John Freeborn's life, but rather a glimpse into a young man's life at a time when Britain stood alone against hundreds of enemy aircraft attempting to pave the way for a German invasion upon her shores. The opinions expressed in this book regarding certain events and characters, which may be deemed as controversial, are of course John's alone, as this author did not know of circumstances surrounding said events or the people involved personally.

My intentions for this book were of course to highlight a period in John's life that is both historic and sought after, but mainly in an attempt to capture the true character of John Freeborn and to illustrate how he personally viewed his time with 74 Squadron during such a conflicted time.

This work has been an absolute labour of love and I am greatly honoured to have been given the opportunity to write about my dear friend and hero, John Freeborn.

It is with my greatest hopes that the reader is made aware of the many sacrifices made by those valiant young men who served their country in order to preserve the freedoms we enjoy today.

> *Never in the field of human conflict was so much owed by so many to so few.*
>
> Winston Churchill

Christopher Yeoman
2008

Illustration by David Pritchard

Bibliography

Battle over Britain F.K. Mason (1969)
A Tiger's Tale Bob Cossey (2002)
Tiger Squadron Ira Jones (1954)
Sky Tiger Norman Franks (1980)
I Fear No Man Doug Tidy (1972)
Best of the Few Michael Robinson (2001)
Smoke Trails in the Sky Anthony Bartley (1984)
The Blue Arena Bob Spurdle (1995)
The Blitz: Then and Now - Edited by Winston G. Ramsey (1990)
Fighter Boys Patrick Bishop (2003)
RAF Biggin Hill Graham Wallace (1957)
So Few David Masters (1945)
74 Squadron Operation Record Book Public Records Office, Kew, UK.
74 Squadron Combat Reports

Aircraft flown by John Freeborn

Compiled by Wilf Crutchley

Aircraft	Unit
Tiger Moth	EFTS
Super Fury	8FTS
Hawker Hart	8FTS
Hawker Audax	8FTS
Puss Moth	74 SQN
Gloster Gladiator	74 SQN
Gloster Gauntlet	74 SQN
Fairey Battle	74 SQN
Supermarine Spitfire MKI	74 SQN
Supermarine Spitfire MKII	74 SQN
Miles Master	CFS
Miles Magister	57 OTU
P47 Thunderbolt	USA
Lockheed Lightning	USA
P51 Mustang	USA
Lockheed Havoc/Boston	USA

Aircraft	Unit
B24 Lockheed Liberator	USA
North American Harvard	USA
North American Mitchell 1	USA
B17 Flying Fortress	USA
Supermarine Spitfire VB	602 SQN
Supermarine Spitfire VB	118 SQN
Supermarine Spitfire VI	118 SQN
Supermarine Spitfire VII	118 SQN
Netheravon Dakota	–
Bristol Blenhiem	–
Beechcraft Bonanza	–
Piper Super Cub (4 Seater)	–
6 SQN Hawker Hurricane	286 WING
14 & 87 SQN Martin Marauder	286 WING
22 SQN Bristol Beaufort	286 WING
87 SQN Supermarine Spitfire VC	286 WING
221 SQN Vickers Wellington XIII	286 WING
249 SQN Supermarine Spitfire VB	286 WING
253 SQN Supermarine Spitfire V	286 WING
255 SQN Bristol Beaufighter	286 WING
284 SQN Vickers Warwick	286 WING
416 SQN Supermarine Spitfire VB	286 WING
608 SQN Lockheed Hudson V	286 WING
1435 SQN Supermarine Spitfire IX	286 WING
Italian Cant Z506/S	286 WING
Fiat C42 Falco	286 WING

Index